INTERNATIONAL LABOR LEGISLATION

STUDIES IN HISTORY, ECONOMICS AND PUBLIC LAW

EDITED BY THE FACULTY OF POLITICAL SCIENCE
OF COLUMBIA UNIVERSITY

Volume XCI] [Number 2

Whole Number 208

INTERNATIONAL LABOR LEGISLATION

BY

IWAO FREDERICK AYUSAWA

AMS PRESS
NEW YORK

COLUMBIA UNIVERSITY
STUDIES IN THE
SOCIAL SCIENCES

208

This Series was formerly known as
Studies in History, Economics and Public Law.

Reprinted with the permission of Columbia University Press
From the edition of 1920, New York
First AMS EDITION published 1969
Manufactured in the United States of America

Library of Congress Catalogue Card Number: 75-82244

AMS PRESS, INC.
NEW YORK, N. Y. 10003

To

MARGARET LORING THOMAS

PREFACE

This is a study of the history and progress of international labor agreements, treaties, conventions and congresses, resulting in labor legislation with international validity or important international bearings. In its preparation the writer received help from a large number of kind people. It was their friendship which made the publication of this monograph possible.

The writer is particularly indebted to Professors Samuel M. Lindsay and Henry R. Seager for their encouragement and guidance. They have given him unstintedly of their precious time in directing the research and examining the manuscript of this work. Acknowledgment must be made to Mr. K. Shidehara, Ambassador Plenipotentiary and Extraordinary of Japan at Washington for the personal interest he has taken in this work. Dr. John B. Andrews, Mr. Alexander Trachtenberg and many others are also gratefully remembered. Especially is the writer under great obligation to Mr. K. Kumasaki, Japanese Consul General in New York for appointing him to attend the Washington Conference of 1919 and also to Dr. M. Oka, former Director of Commerce and Industrial Affairs, Japan, for enabling the writer to attend in various capacities important sessions of the International Labor Conference at Washington.

The help and interest of Mrs. Edward Thomas have been an ever-present inspiration. They will be long remembered with gratitude and deep appreciation.

CONTENTS

PART I

Historical Background

CHAPTER I

PAGE

Origin and Development of International Labor Legislation (1818–1890)

CHAPTER II

Progress Toward International Agreements on Labor (1890–1900)

PAGE

CHAPTER III

International Labor Conferences and Treaties (1900–1913)

CHAPTER IV

World War, Peace Conference and Labor Charter (1914–1919)

PART II

Difficulties in International Labor Legislation

CHAPTER V

Analysis of the Difficulties

CHAPTER VI

Varied Industrial Conditions

PART III

An Attempt to Solve Difficulties in International Labor Legislation

CHAPTER VII

Washington Conference of 1919

PAGE

CHAPTER VIII

Washington Conference—Continued

PART I
HISTORICAL BACKGROUND

CHAPTER I

Origin and Development of International Labor Legislation

1. *The beginning of world-wide labor legislation*[1]

In October, 1919 the first International Labor Conference under the League of Nations was convoked by President Wilson of the United States and began the work of making world-wide the liberal labor laws of the more advanced nations. The Conference met at Washington[2] with representatives of more than forty nations,[3] the delegates representing not private associations and individuals who are merely "interested," as has been the case heretofore in the conferences of similar description, but the governments of the "high contracting parties" to the Covenant of the League of Nations as well as organizations of employers and workers in all the countries where such were in existence.[4] Thus began the organized effort to dissipate the fears of trade competition from countries with lower standards which have for generations obstructed the progress of labor protection along international lines.

[1] *Cf.* Mahaim, *Le Droit International Ouvrier*, pp. 183-203; Chatelain, *La Protection Internationale Ouvriere*, chs. ii, pp. 9-65; Adler, *Die Frage des Internationalen Arbeiterschutzes IX*, pp. 65-113; Fontaine, "La Legislation Internationale du Travail" in *Revue Politique et Parlementaire*, vol. lxxix, pp. 225-230; Lowe, *International Aspects of Labor Problem*, ch. i; Boilley, *La Legislation Internationale du Travail*, ch. i.

[2] The Conference lasted from October 29-November 29, 1919.

[3] See chapter vii.

[4] See Part XIII of the Peace Treaty. Article 389.

Limited as was the number of subjects which the conference took up for consideration,[1] the problem with which it dealt was none the less of fundamental social and international significance. In the absence of any super-legislature, which alone could make the decisions of such a conference effectively binding, and owing to the fact that the League of Nations legally was still non-existent, the conference labored under a considerable handicap. Nevertheless, inasmuch as the members had previously agreed to submit, within a year of its adoption, the final draft of conventions and other decisions of the conference to the properly functioning bodies of each country for their legislative deliberation,[2] such conventions and decisions were bound to be of far more import than those of any previous conference. Whether or not those six draft conventions and nine recommendations will be adopted by the parliaments without serious objection and enforced effectively by the "competent authorities" of different countries are questions which remain to be answered. But as the direct result of the Washington conference, and as the Treaty of Versailles had contemplated,[3] the International Labor Office has begun to function as the central world agency for the collection and publication of information in regard to both the successes and failures of different governments to conform to the official standards of labor protection set up and agreed to by the International Labor Conference.

Thus it appears that labor has for the first time in its history been assured of world-wide legislative protection. Modest as was the program of the conference, its decisions are affecting the lives of millions of the industrial population on all the continents of the earth.

[1] *Cf.* Annex to Part XIII of the Peace Treaty.

[2] Art. 405 fifth paragraph of the Peace Treaty.

[3] Articles 388-396 of the Peace Treaty.

Upon examination of the proceedings of the conference and especially upon analysis of the problems to which the conference devoted much of its time, we realize the magnitude of the questions with which an international conference of this kind will always be confronted. Their solution through the progress of international labor protection in the future must depend largely upon thorough knowledge, derived from careful study and analysis of the difficulties which have always beset the course of conferences of a similar nature in the past. Upon this ground we shall first of all trace briefly the origin and development of the movement in the direction of international labor legislation.

2. The genesis of the idea:[1] *Robert Owen (1771-1858)*

Like the underlying ideas of all social movements which have later swept the continents of Europe and America with their far-reaching waves of moral influence, the idea of the protection of labor may be traced back for many centuries to the genius and idealism of more than one individual. But the specific and concrete idea of international labor regulation is a comparatively recent development. In fact, the history of the movement toward any form of international legislation on labor conditions covers only a few generations.

It is an interesting fact to our mind that it was almost on the one hundredth anniversary of the historical effort of Robert Owen—to whom the honor of originating this particular matter must be ascribed—that the plan for the first International Labor Conference under the League of Nations was launched.

[1] Chatelain, chs. ii-iii; Mahaim, pp. 183, *et seq.*; Lowe, ch. i; G. C. Tabacovici, *De la legislation internationale du travail* (Paris, 1896), pp. 69-70; Benoit Nalon, *Socialisme integral, 2e partie* (Paris, 1892), p. 72; also *La Revue socialiste* (December, 1890), pp. 643-644, "La Legislation internationale du travail."

Precisely a century and a year's time had elapsed when the Washington Conference met since the appearance of the memorials of that great social reformer, Robert Owen, before the Congress of the Holy Alliance at Aix-la-Chapelle. There he went in the year 1818[1] to the great assembly of the potentates of Europe and expounded to as many as he met the proposition that "as the unaided deliberations of governments are necessarily slow and the people are daily injured by the effects of the new scientific power . . . with a view to accelerate the execution of the object which the allied powers must have so much at heart,"[2] he would submit to the congress that "the prime task for the governments of Europe was the international fixation of the legal limits of normal industrial conditions for European society."[3] From September 20 to October 22 of the same year he issued two series of memorials with appendices—"on behalf of the working classes," the first presented to the governments of Europe and America, the second to the allied powers assembled in Congress at Aix-la-Chapelle. The French and German translations of these were soon published as well as the English text. He maintained that "any attempt to stop or retard the introduction of these measures will be unavailing. Already the principles and consequent practices are placed effectually beyond the power of human assault. It will be found that silence cannot retard their progress and that opposition will give increased celerity to their movements."[4] He further stated that "all that the human race requires to secure permanently its

[1] Padmore, *Life of Robert Owen*, ch. xi, p. 253.

[2] *Life of Robert Owen*, supplementary appendix to vol. i, pp. x-xii and 209-222.

[3] Lowe, *op. cit.*, p. 5.

[4] Closing paragraph of the First Memorial, see pp. 209-222 of *Life of Robert Owen*.

health and happiness is to be peaceably well educated and to be continually well employed or occupied alternately, physically and mentally, but never overexercised in either respect."

The views of Owen were thus "characterized," as Miss Hutchins[1] states, "by extraordinary optimism and a pathetic conviction that society was in actual fact, moving rapidly to a state of harmony and coöperation." He also showed "curious ignorance" of certain facts of recent history and made dogmatic assumptions, but the force of his arguments was undeniably felt even by the benighted dignitaries who constituted the ruling classes of Europe in his day. However, the unique petition of this single individual from far-away Scotland had but little effect upon the Congress. The Holy Alliance was too interested in the suppression of national revolts and liberal manifestations. The suggestion was manifestly premature for both the minds and conditions of the time. Before there could be international regulation of labor, there was, in the minds of many statesmen, more urgent need of domestic legislation for the maintenance and aggrandizement of nationalistic interests. The idea of labor protection itself was still undeveloped.

When the matter was still untouched by legislators, William II of Prussia is said to have been favorably impressed with the foregoing proposition of Owen, but Frederick of Gentz, who was the moving spirit of the Holy Alliance, stated to Owen with brutal frankness, as it is recorded:[2] "We do not wish the people to become independent and comfortable. How can we be the rulers if they did?"

Owen's voice was thus unheeded, like the voice of one

[1] Fabian Tract No. 166. *Robert Owen: Social Reformer*, by B. L. Hutchins, p. 21.

[2] *Life of Robert Owen*, ch. i, p. 183 in *Geschichtliche Motive des Internationalen Arbeiterschutzes*, by S. Bauer.

crying in the wilderness; no practical results ensued. Many years after this, in 1857, a little before his death, he issued another memorial with the title " a Letter addressed to the potentates of the earth in whom the happiness and misery of the human race are now vested; but especially to Austria, France, Great Britain, Russia, Scandinavia, Turkey, and the United States of America; because these powers are now at peace with each other and could without war easily induce all the other governments and people to unite with them in practical measures for the general good of all through futurity." [1]

In this he made a definite suggestion that in May of the following year an international world congress be held in London, to which the leading governments of the world, including even those of China, Japan, Burma, *etc.*, should be invited. He declared that he would there unfold to the congress the natural means by which the people may " with ease and pleasure gradually create those surroundings in peace and harmony, which shall have a perpetual good and superior influence upon all."

This proposal suffered much the same fate as every one of his preceding propositions, but his life-long agitation and extensive lecturing tours throughout the continent and in England were not without effect. In spite of the harsh criticisms and adverse contentions [2] of those who held that such schemes as were proposed by Owen were Utopian and destructive of the economic security of the national life, much protective legislation followed in course of time. England led the way in enacting labor laws, limiting the employment of children in textile mills and protecting the workers in various ways. Europe followed suit.[3]

[1] *Life of Robert Owen*, supplementary appendix to vol. i, x-xii.

[2] For an interesting account of the rise of protective labor laws, *cf.* B. L. Hutchins, *History of Factory Legislation*, pp. 1-43.

[3] See Mahaim, pp. 6-8.

3. *Daniel Legrand (1783-1859)*

There are a few prophetic figures whose names must appear in connection with that of Owen in the first chapter of any history of international labor legislation. The first and preëminently the most notable is that of an Alsatian, Daniel Legrand, a silk manufacturer in the town of Steinthal, who early saw the limitations of natonal legislation in the matter of adequate labor protection and formulated plans for international coöperation. During the years 1840 to 1847 he addressed the governments of Europe, urging them to consider this matter which alone could furnish an effective and proper basis of labor protection. "*Il y a*," he said in his memorial,[1] "*dans l'état actuel de l'industrie européene, certains faits que les nations isolement, individuellement ne peuvent régler, qui ne le seront que par un accord des puissances qui y sont interessées.*" His first note was addressed to the ministry of France and to the members of the Council at Paris, demanding that an international conference be called in order to legislate on the protection of the workers. His proposition received but scant attention at the time. Later he again wrote a note "on behalf of the suffering classes who are so worthy of constant solicitude of the governments and so intimately and legitimately connected with the destinies of princes and peoples," and sent it to the cabinets of Berlin, St. Petersburg, Paris and Turin. He maintained in this note that "an international law governing industrial activities is the only possible solution of the great social problem, of according to the working classes the desirable moral and material benefits without which industries suffer and the competition of manufacturers of different nations escapes the necessary restraint." He laid out

[1] Chatelain, p. 10, *et seq.*; also "Un Precurseur du Droit International Ouvrier" in *La Revue Generale du droit international public*, by Krawtschenko, pp. 221-225.

detailed plans for international coöperation which alone, as he maintained, could thoroughly ameliorate the conditions of the workers.[1] He said that three things at least must be done in order to achieve reform, namely: (1) the employment of children must be prohibited; (2) one day of rest out of seven must be assured to all workers; (3) every worker must be assured the opportunity to enjoy family life.

Pointing to the chief industrial evils, which he enumerated as, "(a) lack of education, (b) employment of immature youths in the workshops, (c) excessive labor, (d) night work, (e) Sunday work followed by '*debauché*' on Monday, (f) mingling of sexes, (g) keeping the workers in barracks, (h) neglecting aged workers," he urged that they might be remedied by (1) prohibiting first of all the work of male children under ten years of age and of females under twelve; (2) limiting their work to six hours in twenty-four until thirteen years of age; (3) lengthening the work-day to ten hours upon their attainment of the age of fourteen, with provision for at least an hour's recess for lunch; (4) prohibiting Sunday or night work for young people under 18 and for women and girls of all ages; (5) regulating works which involve unhealthy or dangerous processes; (6) limiting the work of adults to twelve maximum hours a day, which shall begin no earlier than 5:30 in the morning and shall never last after 8:30 in the evening; (7) requiring proper certificate of the age, school, and employment records of young employees, *etc.*[2]

This letter with its appealing and vigorous idealism was sent out four successive times during the years 1853-1857 to the statesmen of European governments,[3] but in spite of this repeated appeal it brought no fruitful response.

[1] *Archives diplomatiques 1890* (2 Serie) XXXVI, pp. 36-40.

[2] *Cf.* Chatelain, pp. 10-12, and Lowe, pp. 7-8.

[3] Krawtschenko, p. 223.

4. *Jérome Blanqui (1798-1854)*

No account of the origin of internationalism in labor legislation is complete without mention of the name of the liberal economist Blanqui, a contemporary of both Owen and Legrand, who sounded a call for international action on behalf of labor, in his course of lectures. His views, which were propounded in his *Cours d'économie industrielle,* have been collected and published with full annotation by Adolphe Blaise.[1] According to Blanqui, the only means of avoiding disastrous industrial abuses and of bettering social conditions of maladjustment was to let all industrial peoples come to an agreement and adopt uniform measures. Of course, he admitted the difficulty of carrying out such a program, but at the same time he firmly believed in its practicability because as he held there is "no reason why men will not unite for the conservation of life as they do for its destruction." [2] This view, however, was after all that of an academic man; it long remained merely an interesting example of academic speculation.

In contrast with the academic view of Blanqui, important practical suggestions and work were contributed by Villermé, another French contemporary of the precursors of this movement already mentioned.

Beginning in the year 1833, at the request and under the auspices of the Academy of Moral and Political Sciences, he made an inquiry into working conditions in the textile industry. His report, which came out in 1839, may be seen in the famous *Tableau de l'état physique et moral des ouvriers employés dans les manufactures de coton, de laine et de soie,*[3] a report in two volumes presenting in full detail the frightful conditions of industry at that time.

[1] Paris, 1838–1839, pp. 119-121.

[2] Krawtchenko, pp. 221-222; Bauer, *Geschichtliche Motive*, p. 94.

[3] Paris, 1840, 2 vols.

This, after all, was the period only of vain desires and fruitless efforts, but once the fire of hope was kindled it was not long before national legislation was enacted in several countries, although a few decades had yet to elapse before international action was attempted. Laws were passed in England, France and other industrial countries step by step in the interest of the working population.[1]

5. *The first official move by the Swiss Canton of Glarus (1855) and the developments in France, Germany,* etc. *(1855-1871)*

Next in importance to the date 1818, which marked the beginning of the movement for international labor legislation with that memorable incident at Aix-la-Chapelle, is the year 1855, more than a generation subsequent to the first of the fruitless endeavors of Robert Owen. The year 1855 is important because it marks the beginning of the official, as contrasted with the private, move toward international action. On September 26 of that year the canton of Glarus, which had for the first time elaborated its factory legislation, as the result of an inquiry made by a commission, wrote to the Council of Zurich, asking it to agree to a plan for labor protection upon an international basis. The report of the commission suggested the need of an international concordat to regulate the length of the workday, child labor, *etc.*, but it expressed at the same time the apprehension that an attempt to create a uniform system among all the industrial nations of Europe might, for the time being at least, be classified in the category of "vain hopes." However, the report strongly urged that it was all the more the duty of the moment to strive for greater uniformity in a more limited sphere.[2]

[1] Alfred (S. Kidd), *History of Factory Movement,* 1857. For brief account *cf.* Mahaim, pp. 7-11.

[2] The report states . . . "mais comme cette idée rentre dans tous les

This project was not taken up,[1] but the following year (1856) a Bavarian by the name of Hahn submitted a plan for an "international law relative to industrial work" at the *Congrés international de bienfaisance* at Brussels. The idea of Hahn was received favorably and the following year (1857) the congress of Frankfort took up the same matter and adopted it with general approbation.

In *L'industrie contemporaine, ses caractères, ses progrès chez les differents peuples,* a book which appeared in 1856, written by Audiganne, is found an argument setting forth the need of international industrial law. "*Pourquoi,*" he says among other things, "*á une époque ou les échanges internationaux se multiplient chaque jour, le droit industriel n'aurait il pas les siens? L'unité de cette partie des lois chez les nations civilisées serait un progres au point de vue chretien et au point du vue social.*" [2]

Soon thereafter, by the publication of Bluntschli's *Dictionary of Political Science* in 1858, the same idea was given far-reaching publicity, and from this time on there was an ever-widening agitation for and awakening of public interest in agreements in reference to protective labor laws among nations.[3] The cause found its able protagonists in such thinkers as Braber and Bluntschli, who advocated Sunday rest and other practical measures. Adolph Wagner and Luijo Bretano, later to become leading professors of political economy in Germany, responded with

cas pour le moment dans la categorie des vains desirs, on ne devrait au moins pas reculer devant la tentative de supprimer autant que possible les diversites dans une sphere officielle aux memes principes." *Cf. Archives diplomatiques,* XXXVI, pp. 40-41.

[1] *Actes de la Conference diplomatique pour la protection ouvriere,* reunie a Berne, du 17 au 18 septembre, 1906, Berne 1906, p. 9. See Mahaim, p. 197.

[2] Mahaim, p. 197.

[3] Chatelain, p. 13; Lowe, pp. 8-9.

no less enthusiasm. The former had already declared his support of the idea in his lectures in 1864. His *Rede über die Soziale Frage,* published in 1871, contained arguments for labor protection by international agreements in such manner as would not be injurious to the industrial life of the nation. In Brentano's *Handbuch der Politischen Oekonomie* are found the programs for the total prohibition of Sunday labor, the suppression of the employment of minors and married women, limiting of hours of work, and internationalization of labor legislation.

6. *The rise of the First Internationale (1866)* [1]

In recounting the rise of internationalism in labor legislation, the latent significance of the revolutionary project of the Internationales must not be overlooked even though our aim primarily is only to outline the course of legislative and remedial attempts rather than the revolutionary movements as such.

In November, 1847, still in the lifetime of Owen and his associates, when the industrial and social conditions in England and in Europe had about reached the stage of intolerable maladjustment, a workingmen's association, a secret society, first exclusively German, but remodeled later upon an international basis and known as the Communist League, held its congress in London.[2] In January of the following year, as one result of decisions reached at this congress, was issued the Communist Manifesto, written by Karl Marx and Friedrich Engels, declaring to the world the revolutionary philosophy and principles of the down-

[1] *Cf. L'internationale, documents et souvenirs,* 1864-1878, 1-4 by James Guillaume, Paris, 1905; Kirkup, *History of Socialism,* ch. viii; *Die international Arbeiterassociation, ihre Geschichte, Programm und Thätigkeit,* by Karl Hillmann, Hamburg, 1871.

[2] *Socialism of To-day* by Wm. E. Walling and associates, p. 3.

trodden, fettered proletariat. The manifesto first came out in German, was circulated a few weeks before the French revolution of February 24, and was published in French and brought to Paris shortly before the June insurrection of 1848. The central board of the League was established in Cologne, to push actively propaganda of the doctrines outlined in the Manifesto, in order ultimately to unite the forces of the proletariat of all the nations upon the common ground of the unity of interest of all working people. The defeat of the Parisian insurrection served, however, apparently to check the spread of radicalism for a brief period.[1]

But the force of might which subdued the Parisian mob, without eradicating the fundamental evils of the industrial fabric, was inadequate to check for long the spread of the human impulse of the workingmen to rise and better their own conditions. In 1864 the International Workingmen's Association was formed in London with the express purpose of welding into one body the whole militant working population of Europe and America. The association, however, could not at once proclaim the principles of the Manifesto. To amalgamate into one the slow English trades unions, the intellectual followers of Proudhon in France, Belgium, Italy and Spain, and the intelligent Lassallians in Germany, the program to be adopted had to be broad and indefinite enough to be acceptable to all.[2]

This International Workingmen's Association, known as the Internationale, held its first meeting at Geneva in 1866, a conference mainly of trade-unionists representing different countries. The thing which we regard as significant

[1] *Communist Manifesto.* Introduction written by Friedrick Engels, January 30, 1888, in London, pp. 1-5. See also, *L'alliance de la Democratie socialiste et l'association internationale des travailleurs*, I-II, pp. 1-15.

[2] See Engel's introduction to the *Communist Manifesto*, p. 4.

for this brief historical sketch is the series of resolutions formulated there and to be included thereafter among the demands of labor, a program touching upon many fundamental aspects of the international labor movement.

The workers were to demand the limitation of the hours of the standard work-day, exclusive of necessary operations in certain industries, for all laborers, and the prohibition of night work; prohibition of the gainful employment of children between 9 and 13 years; the limitation of the working hours of older children; and the prohibition of night work for women and of all work injurious to the health of the worker. Finally the association demanded that the governments take steps to bring about international labor protection.[1] In all its subsequent meetings the association stood as the proponent of international labor laws and issued demands and proposals persistently, which however did not attain fruition until many years later.

Since this organization stimulated and accelerated the progress of the protective movement, a brief mention of each of its subsequent meetings will not be superfluous. The second meeting of the Internationale was held at Lausanne in 1867, where the association adopted programs which were "distinctly socialistic." The next one that was held was at Brussels in 1868. The 1869 meeting at Basel was the first at which there was a representative from the United States among the delegates.[2] It was here also that Bakunin and his anarchist associates were admitted into the association. There was a meeting at London in 1871 and at the Hague in 1872. It was on the latter occasion

[1] Chatelain, p. 13.

[2] See *Documentary History of American Industrial Society*, by Commons and Andrews, vol. ix, pp. 43-46, 338, cited by Lowe. The American National Labor Union sent A. C. Cameron as its delegate to the Basel Convention. See *Association Internationale des Travailleurs*, compte rendu du IVe Congres, Bruxelles, 1869, p. xi.

that the split in the association came about and the expulsion of the more radical anarchistic element resulted, foreshadowing the disruption of the organization. In 1872 the general council was removed to New York where it survived barely two years. Some time later the anarchists met at St. Imier. The Geneva meeting of socialists, in 1894, marks the end of the First Internationale.

7. *Further progress of the movement (1871-1885) and the second official move by Switzerland*

While attaching much importance to the conferences which are the expression of organized effort in the movement, one must not overlook the efforts of men whose individual opinions were of help to the cause. In this connection one must note the name of Louis Wolowski, who published in his *Le travail des enfants dans les manufactures* [1] very liberal views on the subject. The point he brought out clearly was that if the exploitation of women, children and young people was rendered necessary by foreign competition, those evils should be done away with by an international agreement in the same manner as the slave trade had been abolished. In 1873 he made a definite suggestion to the French National Assembly as to international labor agreements. The same proposition was repeated by J. B. Dumas the following year, who submitted a definite plan to the assembly. Besides the names of Wolowski and Dumas, those of Schoenberg and Thiersch in Germany should be noted. Schoenberg, in his *Arbeitsämter*, has gone into the question of international labor legislation. Thiersch was a theologian who took up the idea of Legrand and appealed to the German emperor to call an inter-

[1] *Leçons de L. Wolowski*, avril, 1868, Paris, pp. 14-17. Cited by Chatelain, p. 14.

national labor conference. It was in 1871 that Schoenberg's work appeared, but a thing of even more interest which happened that year was the proposal made by Bismarck to the Comte de Beust that Germany and Austria hold a conference in order to formulate the basis of an international agreement for social legislation between these two countries. As the result of this proposal a conference was called at Berlin from November 7 to 9, 1874, but no concrete agreement was reached.

The appearance of *Die Frage des internationalen Arbeiterschutzes* belongs to a little later date (1888) but the significant efforts of its author, George Adler, must at least be referred to here in mentioning the names of individuals who contributed toward the progress of this cause.[1] The Lyons Congress of French Socialists in 1877 passed resolutions in favor of international protection, and then in 1879 the Christian manufacturers in the regions north of Lille declared that the governments can, and should, regulate the labor situation along international lines. The Paris Congress of the Socialists in 1881 passed a similar resolution.[2]

A little before this, in 1876, a second official move in the direction of international labor legislation was started by the Swiss Republic. Colonel Frey, then President of the Republic, formerly minister to the United States, in his address before the national chamber declared that there was every reason for Switzerland to call for an international conference to bring about adequate and uniform labor regulations.[3] In 1800 the same view was crystallized and presented again by him in the form of a definite motion

[1] Chatelain, pp. 39-58.

[2] Mahaim, p. 199.

[3] See *Archives diplomatiques*, 1890, vol. xxxvi, p. 41. Also *Actes de la conference de Berne*, p. 10.

on December 9 before the Chamber directing the Federal Council to enter into negotiations with the principal industrial nations with a view to establishing international factory regulations. This motion was taken up for consideration on April 20, 1881, and its adoption led to the second official move by Switzerland for international labor legislation. The Swiss government approached the governments of Germany, Austria, Belgium, France, England and Italy through its diplomatic representatives. The proposition, however, aroused no interest and the project failed. From this time on, nevertheless, the agitation was fairly continuous and the time was ripening. No conference met without making urgent demands in this direction. Preëminent among the conferences of this period were the Hygiene Conference of Brussels in 1880, the Paris Congress of Workingmen in 1883 and the socialist congress at Roubaix in 1884.

At this Roubaix congress, resolutions were drafted relating to the need of international legislation prohibiting the employment of children below 14, and night work except in certain absolutely necessary processes, limiting the work-day of men and women, safeguarding their health and finally fixing the minimum wage of the workers.[1]

8. *Developments in France (1885-1889), the Second Internationale (1889), and the third official move by the Swiss government.*

Before the Chamber of Deputies at Paris the following year (1885), Vaillant took up the same matter which had been presented the previous year by Count Albert de Mun. The proposal of de Mun, as expressed in his address, was adopted in an order of the day requesting the government to prepare for international legislation for the protection

[1] Chatelain, p. 16.

of workmen, and their wives and children, in each country in such a manner as not to endanger the national industry.[1] The contention of Vaillant was that industrial evils should be combated internationally, and that the experience of international commercial treaties afforded a basis for international labor laws, which might be supplemented in each country by special labor laws. He recognized the fact that the truth of the essential complaints of the proletariat, as expressed by their leaders in different countries, had long been admitted, and he argued that the self-interest of employers should not be allowed to obstruct international labor agreements, since these were a step toward decreasing industrial crises and insuring greater commercial and industrial stability which would be of advantage to both the workers and employers.

His arguments had a decided effect upon this legislature, for in December of the same year the leading deputies, such as Proudhon, Camelinat, Boyer, Hugues, Basley and Gilly submitted a bill to the council relating to international labor legislation and favoring the action of the Swiss government. It was an endeavor to bring about an international concordat for the abolition of child labor, under the age of 14, the installation of hygienic and safety measures, establishment of accident insurance, weekly rest-day, normal working hours, regular inspection of workshops, limitation of work of women and children, and finally the establishment of an international labor bureau to collect and publish statistical information. In the meantime, while France was showing such progress, the prospect in Germany was by no means encouraging.

On January 25, 1885, the proposal of Baron Hertling, who rose in the Reichstag to champion the cause of international labor laws, and aroused heated debate by his en-

[1] *Op. cit.*, p. 17.

thusiasm, was dealt a mortal blow by the appearance of the Iron Chancellor, who condemned the plan as "impossible and impracticable." [1]

In the summer of the following year (1886) the problem of a normal work-day was the topic of discussion at an international labor conference which met at Paris. It issued a resolution urging the workers of all countries to demand that their governments enter into international agreements on labor protection. In 1887 the Congress of Trade Unionists of France, which met at Montluçon, responded to this appeal and urged the government to negotiate with other countries for labor protection.

On October 23, 1887, a proposition of the same nature was made by Favon, a socialist, and Décurtins, a Catholic, in the Swiss National Council, that the federal council parley with foreign governments on protective labor agreements.[2] The time was at last ripe and this proposal bore fruit in the convocation of the conference of 1890. Meantime, in the French Chamber, a proposal made by Millerand was adopted. It provided for the nomination of a commission consisting of 22 members in order to study labor legislation as a subject of future international treaties. In this rising tide of labor legislation, the Workingmen's Association which had been disrupted in 1874, was gradually revived, and finally in the year 1889 the first congress of the association, the "Second Internationale" met in Paris on July 14, on the hundredth anniversary of the storming of the Bastille.[3] The congress was attended by no

[1] G. Adler, *Die Frage des internationalen Arbeiterschutzes*, p. 88.

[2] *Archives diplomatiques*, 1890, XXXVI, p. 45, *et seq.*

[3] *Socialism of To-day*, pp. 6-7. For a full account see *Le Mouvement socialiste internationale* by Jean Longuet, in *Encyclopedie Socialiste*, edited by Compère-Morel. See also Kirkup, *History of Socialism*, p. 194.

less than 400 delegates, representing trades unions, and socialist and anarchist organizations of twenty countries. Certain resolutions prepared previously by an international conference held on February 28 of the same year at the Hague were presented to this congress. It declared itself in favor of the Swiss government's move and urged the socialist and labor organizations to unite in their effort to materialize the Swiss plan. The congress further adopted a program including the prohibition of the employment of children under 14, and of night work in general; an eight-hour day; one day of rest in seven; the establishment of international minimum-wage and health standards; the creation of systems of state-paid national and international factory inspection, *etc.*[1]

A month later, the general Council of Bouches du Rhone passed a resolution inviting the government of France to initiate an international negotiation for labor protection limiting the working day to eight hours. The initial step, however, had already been taken by the Swiss Federal Council, which had addressed a circular note to the governments of the leading nations of Europe.[2] This was the proverbial third of the attempts which was to decide their final success or failure. The note anticipated the difficulty of attaining at a stroke all the desired ends of legislative idealism. While it contemplated only a gradual development, it forecast a fruitful outcome in view of the general

[1] This organization henceforth held international conferences every two to four years: Brussels, 1891, Zurich, 1893, London, 1896, Paris, 1900, Amsterdam, 1904, Stuttgart, 1907, Copenhagen, 1910, and Basel, 1912. The special feature of the 1896 congress was the anarchist discussion and that of 1900 the debate on ministerialism. The congress of 1912 was a special peace conference. A congress was to be held in 1914 in Vienna. It was later transferred to Paris, but the outbreak of the War prevented it and the conference was not held as had been planned.

[2] *Arch. dip.* XXXI. pp. 77-79.

trend of progress in this field throughout Europe in the preceding years. As the basis of negotiation, the note presented a program, proposing: (1) prohibition of Sunday labor; (2) prohibition of employment of women and children in dangerous or unhealthy processes; (3) fixation of minimum age of children admissible to industry; (4) fixation of hours of work for young persons; (5) restriction of night work of women and children, *etc.*

The note further suggested the manner in which the conventions adopted should be put into actual operation.

The significant and interesting thing to be noted was the attitude shown by the various governments of Europe toward this note. Of fourteen countries to which the note was addressed, four, *i. e.*, Germany, Denmark, Norway and Sweden sent no reply. Russia flatly refused to participate on the ground of impracticability of enforcement of any law in her vast empire. England and Italy expressed their hesitancy in their replies. Spain only acknowledged the receipt of the note and took no action, and only six, *i. e.*, less than one-half of all, including Austria-Hungary, France, Luxemburg, Belgium, Holland and Portugal, responded in an encouraging manner.

The conference, it was originally intended, was to be held in September, 1880, but the manner of response to the Swiss note suggested the advisability of its postponement. On February 5, 1890, the Swiss government sent formal invitations with detailed programs, but it was intimated therein that the conference was to be of a non-diplomatic character. It was to be convoked on May 5, 1890, at Berne, Switzerland.[1]

[1] Chatelain, pp. 31-39; for a brief account of the development up to this time, see, *Revue politique et parlementaire*, 1914, vol. lxxiv, pp. 225-231.

CHAPTER II

Progress toward International Agreements on Labor

1. *Congress of Berlin (March 15, 1890)* [1]

The first of the international labor conferences ever called together and attended by official representatives of the governments of Europe was *not* convoked by Switzerland and it was *not* held at Berne as had been planned by that country, which had striven for the cause so many years. Switzerland waived the honor for the sake of the cause. It was called by Germany and held at Berlin two months earlier than the date originally contemplated.

The reason for Switzerland's acquiescence and the lead taken by Germany was the sudden appearance of two imperial rescripts addressed by William II of Germany, one to Chancellor Bismarck and the other to Messrs. Berlepsch and Maybach on February 4, 1890.[2] The rescript addressed to Bismark expressed unmistakably the determination on the part of the Emperor "to lend a hand to the betterment of the conditions of the German workers in proportion to the solicitude occasioned by the necessity of maintaining German industry in such a state that it can meet the competition of the international market and insure thereby its own existence and that of the workers as well." [3] The rescript was an explicit recognition by this

[1] Mahaim, pp. 203-210; Chatelain, pp. 58-75; Lowe, pp. 27-30.

[2] *Archives diplomatiques*, 1890, XXXIII, pp. 325-326.

[3] Translation by Lowe, *op. cit.*, p. 24.

benignant sovereign of the fact that an international agreement entered into by the countries of chief industrial importance was the only means of solving, or at least of diminishing, the difficulties of industrial evils caused by foreign competition. It charged Bismarck to approach the governments of Belgium, England, France and Switzerland, through the diplomatic agencies of Germany stationed in those countries, in order to ascertain their readiness to enter upon an international agreement for the alleviation of industrial stress. It further charged the Chancellor to assemble all the interested governments to a conference if the principle received their approval. This was the first time that Bismarck was overruled by the sovereign will of the new and ambitious ruler, William II, a man "full of the most incompatible impulses."

The second rescript contained the declaration of the emperor's policy of protective labor legislation, assuming as he said "the task of protecting the less fortunate classes in the spirit of Christian morality." It dealt with the inadequacy of existing laws and stated the need of early completion of the legislation on workmen's insurance which had been established in 1883. It laid down as "one of the duties of the government," the regulation of the length and conditions of work so as to safeguard the health and material needs of the workers and satisfy their aspirations for social justice. It gave clear recognition of the right of the workers to be heard through representatives in the adjustment of differences between employers and employees. The Emperor at the same time expressed his ambition to make the mines of the state model institutions as regards the protection given to their workers.

Upon receipt of the rescript, Bismarck drafted the necessary official communications. All the powers originally invited by Switzerland were approached, with the exception of Russia whose refusal was expected on the basis of previous experiences. The Holy See was invited by Emperor William himself and Pope Leo XIII responded[1] to the notification with enthusiasm, approving highly of such a step which he declared would result in the relief of the distressed workers and their rescue from reckless exploitation by their employers.

When the Conference assembled, fourteen countries were represented by their official delegates. They were Austria, Hungary, Belgium, Denmark, England, France, Germany, Holland, Italy, Luxemburg, Norway, Spain, Switzerland, and Sweden. The Conference was presided over by Baron Berlepsch, then minister of Commerce and Labor. It lasted fifteen days from March 15 to 29, and was the longest ever held, and unprecedented in its importance.

The preparation, however, was inadequate and the conference was for immediate purposes a failure. There was more platonic generalization about what *ought* to be than practical consideration of what *could* be done. The discussions were on a large variety of subjects such as the age limit of children admitted to workshops, the working hours, prohibition of women's employment before and after child birth, general protection of children and women workers as to their working conditions, employment in dangerous or unhealthy processes of work, Sunday labor and rest-periods, and the giving of longer notice to the workers who were soon to be dismissed. There were expressions of pious opinions on these subjects but the scepticism early shown by Bismarck seemed justified by the reluctance of the representatives to commit themselves to any concrete proposition. They refused to go beyond consultation, discussion and suggestion. The instructions which the repre-

[1] *Archives diplomatiques*, 1890, XXXV, pp. 1819; *Actes de la Conference de Berlin*, official edition, p. 33.

sentatives had received were restrictive. Even the Belgian, British and French delegates had only limited powers and each jealously guarded the "sovereignty" of his country and stressed the "differences in political and industrial conditions."

The final resolution of the conference, if it deserved such designation at all, was only an emasculated recommendation. Even the provision for the execution of the recommendation began with the timorous expression:—"*pour le cas ou les gouvernements donneraient suite aux travaux de la conference, les dispositions suivantes se recommendent* . . . ." etc.[1] There was a hope expressed to the effect that it would be "desirable" to meet again for similar purposes and the recommendation stated in part that a system of inspection of labor, exchange of documents and annual reports, *etc.*, would also be "desirable" but the hopes were not sustained by any promise of realization.

2. *Spread of international action and the Brussels Congress (1891)*

The apparent failure of the Conference of Berlin, from which so little resulted in spite of much talk, furnished the opponents of the movement with ground for criticizing the attempt as futile and impracticable, but failure was only apparent and not real. That august assembly convoked by the sovereign power of the German Empire with representation from all the great nations of Europe was no small propaganda for the cause. On the one hand, each country, the government of Switzerland still taking the lead, was profoundly impressed with the significance of labor legislation,[2] and set itself to the task of improving labor conditions at home through successive labor laws, and, on the other

[1] Mahaim, p. 207.

[2] Hutchins, *History of Factory Legislation*, chs. ix-xi.

hand, there was a marked extension of the field of international action, undertaken not by the governments whose coöperation seemed for the time being ineffectual and impracticable, but by private individuals and unofficial organizations, the operation of which was far less unwieldy.

Indeed the period from 1891 to 1900 marks the last decade of the age of nationalism. The era of internationalism began with the revolutionary international Socialist Congress held at Brussels in 1891.[1] Here was brought about the union of the two opposing socialistic elements which since 1882, had held separate gatherings, with considerable divergence as manifested even at the Paris Congress of the International Workingmen's Association.[2] By unanimous vote the congress resolved to place itself "on the ground of the class struggle in the conviction that there can be no possibility of the emancipation of the working class as long as there are ruling classes." A rebellious note on behalf of the workers was sounded by the young Belgian socialist leader, Emile Vandervelde, who declared: "for the first time revolutionary socialists and trade unionists have found themselves in agreement in proclaiming the necessity of the class struggle. There is a new fact without precedent; the socialists of the entire world are united, according to the words of Karl Marx; 'Proletarians of the world unite.'" Social reform and labor legislation were the two principal matters upon which the congress sought to define the socialist attitude. This was distinctly a labor agitation.

International actions which had little or no direct bearing on labor, outside of purely political, or scientific, coöperative schemes such as the Danube Commission, had already been started as early as 1851 when the first International Sanitary

[1] *Socialism of To-day*, p. 8 and pt. ii, ch. iv.

[2] For brief account of the schism, *cf. Proposed Roads to Freedom* by Bertrand Russell, pp. 58-62.

Congress was held in Paris with twelve nations represented. A convention affecting the navigation of the Mediterranean was executed by five powers. Later, conferences were held in Paris in 1859; Florence, 1867; Vienna, 1874; Washington, 1881; Rome, 1885; Venice, 1892; Paris, 1893 and 1897, *etc.*[1] As early as 1876 the International Congress of Hygiene and Demography was holding meetings with representatives from various European countries at Brussels. Another meeting of this Congress was held in 1887 at Vienna and still another in Paris two years later. In 1891 the seventh meeting of the Congress was held in London, the eighth met in Budapest in 1894 and the ninth in Madrid in 1898.[2]

The International Prison Commission which first met in London in 1872 held its subsequent meetings at Stockholm, 1878, Rome, 1885, St. Petersburg, 1889 and 1892, Paris, 1895, Brussels, 1900, Budapest, 1905, Washington, 1910, *etc.* A conference for the Suppression of Slave Trade was held at Brussels from Nov. 18, 1889, to July 2, 1890, at the invitation of Belgium. An international bureau was set up at Brussels in 1890. A general act was adopted July 2, 1890, by seventeen powers by referendum.

An attempt to enumerate all the names and dates of international conferences which were being held in the interests of commerce and trade, art and science, education, charity and what not, would be futile as well as superfluous for our purpose. Suffice it to mention that they were the manifestations of the awakening spirit of a new internationalism, of which the labor movement was after all only one. Prior

[1] *American Journal of International Law*, vol. i. For the list of official conferences, see pp. 808-817. For unofficial conferences, *cf.* pp. 818-829.

[2] Others of importance were the Berlin conference, 1907, and the Washington conference, 1912.

to 1890, that is up to the opening of the Berlin Congress, there had been, since 1826, at least 75 such official conferences held, and the number was increasing almost in geometric ratio.

In this connection a brief reference, at least, must be made to a successful movement with no less international consequences than any socialist or governmental conference, though it had little direct bearing on labor, and that is the formation in 1863 of a postal union. Vain efforts were being made to achieve a satisfactory international agreement on the matter of mail and postal carriage. Prior to 1863, the whole matter depended upon separate and special treaties between states and inasmuch as each state gave little heed to international facilities, national profit being its only concern, the postage to foreign states was made as heavy as the "traffic would bear." For instance to send a letter from the United States to Australia one had to pay 5 cents, 33 cents, 45 cents, or $1.02 per half ounce, depending upon the route by which the mail was sent.[1]

As the need of international agreement and regulation became more apparent, the efforts of those who felt the necessity most keenly bore fruit and finally a Postal Congress was held at Berne in October, 1874, at which twenty-two states were represented and a General Postal Union was formed. Subsequently, in 1878, this became the Universal Postal Union. New states have since been admitted into the Union and rules have been modified occasionally, facilitating the communication and exchange among nations to an immeasurable degree. No over-statement can be made of the influence which this movement has had in accelerating coöperative internationalism.

To return to the description of more localized actions, in Switzerland, the home of the spirit of international co-

[1]Cited by Sayre, *Experiments of International Government*, p. 19.

operation, the move for further official action had by no means been checked by the failure of the Berlin Congress. At the suggestion of the workers' and employers' organizations, the Federal Council made in 1892 an attempt through the diplomatic agencies in Germany and Austria, to obtain an international agreement regulating the industry of machine embroidery, but this was a failure because of the reluctance of the two governments to take any action on the proposition. Agitation for another attempt was made later in 1895 in the Federal Chamber but, the Council, after having failed so often, did not regard the time as yet ripe.[1]

3. *Zurich Congress of 1893, the rise of the International Coöperative Alliance,* 1895, *and the London Congress of 1896*

While the governmental authorities were thus hesitant and inactive and official coöperation seemed difficult of realization, the leaders of the proletarian movement were ceaselessly at work. A Congress of the Internationale was held in 1893 in Zurich where the adequacy of peaceable parliamentarism was questioned and a general strike of the workers as a means of preventing war was seriously discussed. It was only after a vigorous protest by Bebel, who defended parliamentarism as the "utilization by the proletariat of political rights and legislation *for the conquest of political power*," that the congress found itself in a position to exclude the anarchistic element from the organization. Political action was thus recognized but the final resolution of the Congress explicitly contained this warning: "In no case can political action be used for compromise or for alliances, which would contradict the principles and the independence of socialist parties." It was at this Congress that Liebknecht, who was a recognized leader in the inter-

[1] Chatelain, pp. 76-79.

national socialist movement, delivered his eloquent discourse on the subject of parliamentarism *versus* direct action. He said that there was no such thing as revolutionary change. His theme was "action rather than words." Even with its significant conclusion the wording of the final resolution was not agreeable to the Dutch delegation, whose proposal for an international general strike had been defeated. They declined to subscribe to the resolution of the Congress.[1]

In 1895 an organization with less of the revolutionary restless temper than the Internationale but with as much progressive spirit as any known labor organization, known as the International Coöperative Alliance was formed.[2] Its preliminary conference had been held two years previously (1893) at the Crystal Palace, London. The Alliance, as its program states, was formed "with the object of bringing coöperatives of all communities in touch with one another, so as to enable them to afford one another mutual support, to learn from one another, to discuss in common voice and to act in common so far as may be judged expedient without attempting to interfere in the affairs of any individual association or union of societies."[3] The first congress of the alliance was held in 1895 in London; second, 1896, in Paris; third, 1897, in Delft; fourth, 1900, in Paris; fifth, 1902, in Manchester, *etc.* What the organization proposed to accomplish was decidedly modest and its effect necessarily could not be immediate, but the steady growth of the Alliance in later years was remarkable. Mention may be

[1] See *Protokol des internationalen sozialistischen Arbeiter Congresses* in der Tonhalle Zürich vom 6 bis 12 August, 1893. *Hrsg. vom Organisationskomité*, Zurich, 1894; see also *Socialism of To-day*, pp. 9-10.

[2] *Reports of Proceedings of the International Coöperative Alliance*, nos. 1-5, 8, *etc.*

[3] *Ibid.*, *Principal Resolutions of the International Coöperative Alliance of 1895*, pp. i-x.

made, even at the violation of the chronological order, of the fifth congress held at Manchester which was the best attended of any up to that time. The Alliance had already drawn in 18 countries, counting Germany as one, of Europe, Asia, America and Australia. There were 261 coöperative organizations, associations or national unions of societies. More than 570 members and delegates representing various societies attended the congress. The two main topics of discussion were the housing problem and profit sharing. The congress, for the first time in its history held an exhibition, displaying goods contributed by the coöperative societies of the world and it was considered a signal success, establishing " the fact that coöperative production had made good its position in the world as a productive power, well able to compete in the open market on equal terms with other forms of production." [1]

Besides those we have already referred to, other international conferences that were held during this period were the International Railway Congress which had its fourth meeting in St. Petersburg in 1892, its fifth in London in 1895, and its sixth in Paris in 1900; and the International Actuarial Congress which had its first meeting in Brussels in 1895, its second in London in 1898, and its third in Paris in 1900. The International Congress of Women met first in London in 1899.

These conferences were undoubtedly of great interest and exerted untold influence upon the minds of people in the molding and remolding of their social outlook, but their effect upon labor was only indirect. Before the eventful year, 1900, whence started the new era of internationalism, there met three other important labor conferences which we shall briefly describe.

[1] Introduction to the *Report of Proceedings of the Manchester Congress*, 1905.

The first of these is the International Socialist Congress which met in London in 1896.[1] The outstanding feature of this gathering was the anarchist discussion, characterizing the spirit with which the congress was convoked. A fierce fight was waged between the radical syndicalist elements from France and Holland and the representatives from other countries. The syndicalists sought to secure repudiation by the congress of the Zurich resolution of 1893, but this endeávor was unsuccessful. The congress, however, advocated emphatically " all forms of organized struggle for the conquest of political powers . . . . for the emancipation of the working class." It further declared the seizing of political power as the best means for achieving the emancipation of the enslaved class and for the establishment of the Socialist Republic. .It appealed " to the workers of all countries to unite in a party, separate from all bourgois political parties and to demand adult suffrage and the initiative and referendum nationally and locally," and then finally the Congress declared the emancipation of women to be an inseparable requisite to the freeing of the working class and appealed, to the women of the world to organize with the workers. Although the tone of the congress was thus extremely radical, it was at this congress that the Liebknecht motion was adopted, forever excluding anarchists from the Internationale.

4. *Congress of Zurich, (1897)* [2]

In Switzerland, the source of the farflowing stream of international legislation, there were ever-bubbling springs of action adding to its volume. In 1896, the Swiss govern-

[1] *Report of Proceedings of International Socialist Workers and Trade Union Congress*, London, Twentieth Century Press, 1896. See also *Socialism of To-day*, pp. 11-12.

[2] Chatelain, pp. 79-82.

ment again approached the authorities of Austria, Belgium, France, Germany, Denmark, England, Italy, Holland, Norway, Russia, Sweden and Spain for an international concordat for the establishment of an international statistical labor bureau. The function of the bureau as proposed was simply informational and ministerial, with little or no coercive power save that of collecting from each country all information on labor conditions and the legislative status of industry for wide publication. To this suggestion, however, there came hardly one answer which was affirmative, and the majority of those who responded, indicated more hostility than approval.

The failure of its official approach was followed, nevertheless, by the unofficial move made by Décurtin, in the name of the Swiss Federation of Labor, which called the International Conference for Labor Protection on April 25, 1897. This was the largest in attendance and the most important since the first general trade-union congress held in Paris in 1886. The United States of America was recognized for the first time as one of the powers represented. There were fourteen nations represented there, including Austria-Hungary, Belgium, England, France, Germany, Italy, Holland, Luxemburg, Spain, Switzerland, Poland, Russia and the United States. The conference would have met in 1874 had it not been for a disagreement between the Social democrats and the Christian Socialists in Germany which made their participation and the materialization of the conference at that time possible. Prof. Brentano of Germany was largely responsible for initiating the project of the conference. The work of the committee consisting of Brants, Denis, De Ridder, Strauss and Mahaim, which formulated and brought to fruition the original project for this most successful private conference must be recorded in large letters. This conference was a singular success.

Prof. Mahaim of Liége University, who has worked for this cause for years, and who is an unchallenged authority on the subject of International Labor Legislation, in describing this congress says, that there prevailed a sentiment which he calls "*trève de Dieu.*" [1] There was harmony even between the democrats and Christian socialists.[2]

The program followed by this conference was similar to that of the Berlin Congress, the agenda of the conference being as follows: (1) Sunday work; (2) Work of children and young persons; (3) Work of women; (4) Work of adults; (5) Night work and unhealthy work; (6) Means of labor protection.

The conference considered favorably the propositions of Sunday rest, fixed age-limit for child labor at fifteen, adopted the eight-hour day, or fourty-four hour week for women, and the eight-hour day in general for all adults. As for the fifth and sixth items of the agenda, the conference drew up a series of drastic recommendations which were in brief as follows: First, inspection should cover practically all spheres and branches of productive labor. It was to include both large and small industries, and mines, transportation, and domestic and agricultural undertakings which employ machinery. Women inspectors were to be appointed to inspect where women are employed. Secondly, it advocated the right of employees of both sexes to organize. Interference with this right was to be punished. Thirdly, it stood for universal suffrage, equal, direct and secret, in all elections in order to promote the real political interests of labor. Fourthly, the conference endorsed active propaganda by means of conferences, publications, journals, parliamentary action, *etc.* Fifth, the organization of periodic international conferences presenting simultaneously

[1] Mahaim, p. 211.

[2] *Revue Économique Internationale*, 1904, vol. iii, pp. 319-326 (Mahaim).

the proposal of the same law was advocated. The conference urged the Swiss Federal Council to further its efforts to bring about international labor legislation and to have created an international labor bureau.[1]

5. *Congress of Brussels 1897 and the genesis of the International Association for Labor Legislation*

On September 27 of the same year met the Congress of Brussels, a conference of no less importance than any single assembly that was held previously. The efforts of a single individual, Prof. Mahaim, whose name has already appeared, and which will recur more than once in this history, were largely responsible for this gathering. For the first time the congress assumed the title: the Congress for International Labor Legislation (*Congrés de la Legislation International du Travail*). Those veteran forerunners of the movement who took part in the Berlin Congress, reappeared on the scene, the most prominent of them being Baron Berlepsch, the former Minister of Commerce and Labor of Germany, who was the presiding officer of the Berlin Congress, and who acted in the same capacity at this Congress. Under him, assisting on the presiding staff were, Linder[2] and Herze[3] both of whom were also delegates at Berlin. The German delegation was the most imposing, not only numerically but "qualitatively," as it were, with a formidable array of distinguished scholars and public figures such as Schmoller, Brentano, Mayr, Sombart, Herkner, Hitze and Lieber. From Austria came Philippovich, known for his eloquence ever since the Berlin Congress. France had men of no less distinction. Prof. Charles Gide was unable to attend but there were Yves Guyot, A. Raffalovich, L.

[1] Chatelain, pp. 79-82.

[2] Then vice-chairman of French council of mines.

[3] Then Director-general of Mines of Belgium.

Strauss, Fleury, *etc.*, and among the younger men were Paul Pic and Bourque of the new school. Belgium sent the Christian democrat, Verhaegen. Germany, France and Belgium had thus the heaviest representation.[1]

The order of the day was the consideration of a series of questions previously formulated for the occasion, a method initiated by the Swiss government. The questions asked concerned the evolution and modification of labor laws in different countries since the Berlin Congress, and the possibility of bringing about international labor protection. The practical measures for such legislation in their various aspects such as the regulation of small or domestic industries, the utility of standardizing legislation on unhealthy or dangerous trades, the appropriate means for better and more efficient administration of protective laws, the practicability of publishing international labor statistics by the establishment of an international labor bureau, *etc.*, were considered in their successive order.

The establishment of an international labor bureau was admitted universally to be desirable, but the earnest appeal of the reporter, Hector Denis, proved unavailing because of the divergence of opinion as to the workability of such an office unless it was a private bureau. This project thus fell through but the entire congress was by no means fruitless. It was at this congress that the highly important matter of the suppression of industrial poisons by international agreement was brought forward and for the first time the proposition led to important results, in the prohibition of the use of white lead and white phosphorous.

Despite all that may be said in favor of the accomplishments of this congress, its real achievements were to be seen not in what it did but in what happened later. After the adjournment of the congress, a committee of three, consisting

[1] *Revue Économique Internationale*, 1904, vol. iii, p. 321.

of Prof. Mahaim, Duke Ussel and Brants, was formed to function as a continuation or organization committee, "*de rechercher les moyens de donner une suite au Congrès.*"

It was by this little body, that the idea was hatched of "*avant toute une grande association internationale des amis de la legislation du travail.*" In this prospective association, both the right and left wings were to be included so long as they did not oppose legislative means of improving labor conditions. From January, 1898, the committee labored hard and it was there and then that the future International Association for Labor Legislation was conceived. A draft of the constitution of such an association was made by the committee.

A by-product of the work of this committee and a result of the coöperation of the Belgian minister of Labor, Nysseus, was the publication in 1898 of "*l'Annuarie de la legislation du travail*" which was a cyclopedia of labor laws enacted in 1897. The tentative plan of the International Association was greeted with much enthusiasm by Baron Berlepsch who had already made a trip to France with a similar idea. Subsequently on the occasion of the reunion of eminent economists and statesmen of Germany, he announced the plan and immediately a committee of twenty men including all interested parties was formed. In Belgium a commission was already formed with Denis, Prins, and Verhaegen on it for materialization of the Belgian section and the Belgians had every reason to expect that the proposed association would have its International Bureau situated in Belgium and that its first congress would be held in Belgium. Had it not been for the untimely retirement of Nysseus from the office of Minister of Labor, which was occasioned by political change, such would have been the case.[1] However the century closed,

[1] During July, 1899, a momentous matter in the history of international

with an unexpected series of portentous events, of which we shall treat in the next chapter.

arbitration took place at the Hague. Invited by the Tsar Nicholas of Russia, sixteen nations were assembled at this place to consider the creation of permanent arbitral machinery. On July 28, 1899, the famous Hague Convention was signed by all the sixteen powers. A description of this matter has been omitted here because little was said or even thought about labor as a factor in maintaining international peace.

CHAPTER III

Spread of International Labor Conferences and Treaties; the Berne Conventions of 1906 and 1913

1. *Paris in 1900*

The year 1900 is one of the most eventful and important in the history of the international labor movement. It ushered in the era of internationalism, and the city of Paris, the historial scene of the French Revolution, became the scene of the triumphal entry of the international spirit. For the occasion of the World's Fair, literally thousands upon thousands of people thronged thither from all the corners of the earth and scores of conferences, public and private, national and international, were held in this world center of turmoil and peace making. Naturally it is idle to remark that the international gatherings were most predominant. To mention a few of the more important of them, there was held, to begin with, the International Socialist Congress, then came the first meeting of the International Association for the Legal Protection of Labor, and then the International Congress of Public Assistance and Bienfaisance; the International Congress of Navigation; the International Congress of Arboriculture; the International Actuarial Congress; the International Congress of Comparative Legislation; the International Congress on Private International Law; the International Railway Congress; the International Congress on Chronometry; the International Society of Physicists; the International Coöperative Alliances; the International Congress on Work or Assistance in Time of War; the International Congress of Ornithology; the International Conference for the Teaching of the Social Sciences and countless others of less importance.[1] Bewildered, one might conclude with justice that every organization in existence or about to exist found imperative reasons for meeting in Paris in the year 1900. Paris was the scene of discussion, deliberation, agitation and hopeful turbulence without bloodshed.

Of primary interest to us among the innumerable Congresses assembled then in Paris are the Socialist Internationale and the new Association for the Legal Protection of Labor.

2. *The International Socialist Congress of Paris (1900)*[2]

The Congress, with representatives from more than 35 nations and with such celebrated leaders as Vandervelde, Kautsky, Jaurés, Ferri, Aner, Guesde, *etc.*, present, was an assembly destined to be extraordinary. Even before the Conference began its deliberations, there were already menacing signs of stormy discussion and possible disruption. The fact that the socialist member of the French cabinet, Millerand, had accepted a portfolio without the consent of the French socialists, was the occasion for raging controversy. The main task for the congress was the adjudication of this so-called "ministerial question." After a prolonged discussion, the congress adopted the motion proposed by Kautsky who regarded the participation in the bourgeois cabinet by a socialist party member as a "temporary make-shift" which was a question of tactics and not

[1] See *Amer. Jour. of Int. Law*, vol. i, pt. ii, pp. 818-829.

[2] *Congrès anti-parlementaire internationale*, Paris, 1900, in *Temps Nouveaux*, 1900, pp. 129-342. Also W. E. Walling, *Socialism of To-day*, pp. 12-14.

principles. The congress would recognize its utility, so long as the Socialist minister remained a proper representative of his party. However, as the final wording of the motion states, so soon as the socialist member of the ministry ceases to be a representative of his party, "his entry into the Cabinet becomes a means of weakening rather than of strengthening the proletariat." The congress, further, adopted the amendment proposed by Plechanoff whereby the congress laid it down "that a socialist must resign from a bourgeois cabinet if the organized party declares that the cabinet has in any way acted unfairly in the economic struggle between Capital and Labor." The congress then declared categorically that "the class struggle forbids every kind of alliance with any faction whatsoever of the capitalist class" unless such a coalition was a circumstantial necessity from the point of view of tactics. It was explicitly declared that such coalitions must be reduced to a minimum.

It was at this congress that the birth of a permanent organization took place, in order to perpetuate the work of the international conferences. Emile Vandervelde, who later became a member of the Belgian ministry for National Defense, was made the Chairman and Camille Huysmans the secretary of the newly instituted International Socialist Bureau. The bureau was located at the People's House at Brussels and the work of the bureau was conducted by a body known as "international secretaries" consisting of permanent delegates from each country. Larger nations had two and smaller nations one representative on this secretariat. We shall read of the transfer of the bureau from Brussels to the Hague and the development of its work in the following chapter.

3. *The International Association for the Legal Protection of Labor,*[1] *its formation (1900) and functions*

Millerand, the Minister of Commerce in the French cabinet, whose name has become familiar to us, was an ardent supporter of the international labor legislation movement. He had already spoken before the National Assembly regarding the Belgian proposition of an international labor bureau.

Responding to the suggestions of the committee of three already mentioned, Paul Cauwés, acting as Chairman, and Raoul Jay, acting as secretary, called the congress to meet on July 25-29, in Paris, on the occasion of the World's Fair.[2] Delegates were sent from the United States of America, Austria, Belgium, Australia, New Zealand, Holland, Denmark, Russia, Hungary, Switzerland, Germany, England and Mexico. By far the most important task assumed by the conference was the project of the creation of an international labor bureau. On the first day of the conference there was a commission nominated for the execution of this task. The commission under the chairmanship of Nysseus held daily sessions during the conference. It was by no means an easy undertaking on account of the diverse and opposing views of the members present. Finally on the last day of the conference, after almost every possibility of mutual compromise was exhausted, the committee adopted the draft of a statute upon which all could agree, providing for the formation of a commission with the following representation: President, Scherrer of Switzerland; Members, Baron Berlepsch of Germany, Cauwés of France,

[1] *Bulletin of the International Labor Office,* I, 1-3. *U. S. Department of Labor Bulletin,* no. 9, 1904, pp. 1080-1086.

[2] *Revue économique internationale,* vol. iii, 1904, pp. 326, *et seq.*; *Congrès international pour la protection legale du travailleur tenu à Paris au Musée Social,* du 25 au 28 Juillet, 1900, Paris, 1901, vol. i.

Phillippovich of Austria, Tonolio of Italy and Mahaim of Belgium.[1]

The seat of the association was to be in Switzerland, and thus on July 28, 1900, the "International Association for the Legal Protection of Labor" was born. Prof. Stephen Bauer of the University of Basel who had early been recommended by Phillippovich during the session was nominated in September to act as the secretary of the association. Under his secretaryship, up to date, the association has been functioning admirably, making contributions of immeasurable value to the labor protective movement.

Turning now to the technical aspects of the discussions of the conference, there were three matters to be considered. The first was the legal limitation of the working day. As the maximum working time, the congress seemed to agree upon eleven hours with a gradual reduction to ten hours. The second was night work. The congress as usual expressed the pious opinion that it was undesirable and should be prohibited, but with enough qualifications or exceptions. The third matter was the institution of an inspecting system. That the inspectors' corps should include those who represent the rank and file of laboring men was a rather unique feature of the diversified suggestions made on this topic. On the whole the tone or the consensus of opinion of the congress was that no complete unification of labor legislation in all countries could be attempted and that greater uniformity was to come only by the gradual process of evolution. This view was expressed at the outset of the conference by Prof. Cauwés, who was the first speaker and by the presiding officer of the conference, who spoke next.[2]

[1] Scherrer was Swiss delegate to the conference, a lawyer, formerly president of the congress of Zurich. Baron Berlepsch was a German delegate—former Minister of Labor, president of the Berlin Congress. Cauwès was Professor in the Law Faculty of Paris.

[2] *Revue d'économie politique*, 1901, article by Paul Pic, p. 687, *et seq.*

The functions and structure of the International Labor Office, which is the offspring of this congress, are worthy of our close study. In the first place we should remember that this was a private establishment. Prior to its creation, in the commission which considered it and brought it into being, considerable time was spent in determining whether the office should be official or private. While there was no question as to the desirability of an official coercive power vested in such a bureau, it was seriously apprehended at the same time that an office so constituted would be liable to be involved in political, commercial and other complications. The commission followed then the line of least resistance and made it a private bureau.

The chief function of this office is the collection and publication of the laws of labor protection in different countries. The association through this office endeavors to study the legal and legislative status of labor in all countries, the possibilities of unifying labor legislation internationally and of collecting along uniform lines international statistics of labor.

Upon assuming office, the first thing which Prof. Bauer started was "correspondence with various governments in order to effect a regular remittance of their laws and documents, to persuade the industrial associations and trades unions to intrust the office with the consummation of their wishes as to legislation, to make provisions for a working staff, to enter into relationship and arrange terms with publishers and to find finally a financial basis for regular organized work." Toward the beginning of its financial career (1903) the total annual receipts of the association amounted to only about $8000, the General Secretary receiving only $1,200 a year. However on account of its marvelous prospects the association was able to enlist the support of practically all European governments. Switzerland as the seat of the office voted to it 10,000 francs, the United States $200 to the subsidy for publications. Germany, Italy, Belgium and others followed and " for the purpose of official intercourse, almost every state recommended its ministry of commerce to communicate directly with this International Labor Office."

4. *The progress of the Association; its subsequent meetings at Basel and Cologne (1901-4)* [1]

The salutary effect of the work of an organization of this kind can easily be understood. As Article 2, Section 1-5, of its constitution provided, the association thenceforth served as the world's central agency for bringing together the proponents of labor legislation of the different industrial countries. It has facilitated the study of protective labor laws everywhere, by collecting and publishing information on the subject. It has proven a most effective medium for promoting international labor agreements and above all the international congresses which it has organized have been a perpetual source of impulse and stimulation. As the direct consequence of the formation of this association, there sprang up within a short period various national sections.

In France, *l'Association nationale française pour la protection legale des travailleurs* was formed on March 2, 1901. Professors Cauwés and Jay were principally responsible for the formation of this branch. As its statute (Article 2) definitely states, the association includes all classes and groups of interests. The members were socialists, capitalists, Catholics, Protestants, workers and employers. Its office is in Paris.[2]

In Germany *Die Gesellschaft für Sozial Reform* was

[1] Chatelain, pp. 87-104; Mahaim, p. 216; Lowe, pp. 38-42.

[2] *Revue économique internationale*, 1904, p. 332.

formed. It undertook from the start: the examination of labor questions of national interest; creation of an imperial labor office, and the reform of professional associations in Germany. The membership fee of only 3 marks a year made it easy for all classes of people to connect themselves with the association so that soon there were more than 600 members enrolled. Local sections were established at Breslau, Leipzic, Dresden, Hamburg, and Berlin.

In Austria the political conditions made it difficult to form any organization of this nature. There was a law prohibiting organizations with international affiliation but Phillippovich succeeded in forming one, in spite of the law.

Needless to say that in Switzerland there was little of either difficulty or delay. The plan for organization had been elaborated as early as July 10, 1900, and in 1901 it already had 238 members enrolled. Colonel Frey was the first president and the organization enlisted the support of political societies, chambers of commerce and the canton governments.

The Italian section was formed under the government subsidy, due to the efforts of Prof. Tonolio of the University of Pisa, and 70 members joined immediately. In the Netherlands a section was organized almost before the French had started. It was launched by Kerdyck at Amsterdam with 159 members. The Hungarian section is known as "Social Science Society" and the Belgian section, formed May 29, 1901, provides that only 66 titular members have votes as members in order to maintain political neutrality. Other members are known as "subscribers" without votes. Branches in England, the United States, Spain, *etc.*, were formed later.

During September 27-28, 1901, the first Delegates' Meeting of the international association met at Basel. All of the newly formed national sections except the Hungarian were represented with 38 delegates. The governments of France, Italy, the Netherlands and Switzerland sent their "official delegates." The matters of chief importance decided at this meeting were four in number. The first dealt with the function of the International Labor Office, relative to the study of national laws on unhealthy and dangerous trades and occupations. Inseparably related to this was the second topic which was on the use of white phosphorus in the manufacture of matches and the use of lead (white) as well. That the discussion which took place on this matter was not without its effect will be shown in a later section of this chapter. The third topic was on the employment of women at night. This also led to a concrete result a year later as will be explained. Last but of surpassing importance was a general discussion on the treatment of foreign labor. That employers should assume responsibility for accident, illness or death to immigrant workers and especially that they should secure to foreign workers equal insurance benefits—these were the high principles of international importance which were to be realized in the future.

From the year 1902 the International Labor Office began, as provided for in the constitution, the publication of the labor bulletins in French and German [1] entitled respectively *Bulletin de l' Office international du travail* and *Bulletin des internationalen Arbeitsamtes.*

September 26-27 the following year the association held its second delegates' meeting at Cologne. More interest was taken by the governments in this conference than in the preceding one as was proven by the presence of twenty-two "official delegates" representing ten European nations beside forty-two delegates, from seven national branches.

[1] The English version was started in 1906 entitled "Bulletin of the International Labor Office."

Women's labor at night and the use of poisonous materials in manufactories were the two important matters discussed. No concrete results came about immediately, but a commission was appointed to study the questions and, a year later, September 9-11, 1903, the commission reassembled at Basel after having carried on a year's research.

This little commission meeting of 1903 was of unexpected importance, not because of what it did then and there but on account of its consequences. On the recommendation of the commission, an appeal was made to the Swiss Federal Council to convoke another international conference to consider the feasibility of concurrent prohibition of women's night work and the possibility of prohibiting the use of white lead and phosphorus in industry. The appeal was favorably responded to and an official communication was commenced the following year[1] by the Swiss government with all the nations of industrial importance.

5. *Events of the year 1904: Socialist Labor Congress of Amsterdam; International Labor Treaties and the Third Delegates' Meeting of Basel*

With the advance of time events of international significance affecting the field of labor were multiplying year by year. In 1904 the progress seemed accelerated. A new departure in the direction of international labor legislation was made on April 15, 1904, when the French and Italian governments entered into a treaty whereby equal benefits of legal protection and privileges were assured to the workers of both countries residing in either country.[2] The object of the treaty as specified in its preamble was: (1) To grant to nationals of either country laboring in territory of the

[1] Dec. 30, 1904.

[2] For concise accounts of successive treaties for labor protection see Mahaim, pp. 221-243, 317-325; Chaletain, pp. 193; Lowe, ch. v, on "Protective Labor Treaties."

other reciprocal banking accommodations and advantages of social insurance, and (2) To guarantee the mutual maintenance of protective labor measures and coöperation in the advancement of labor legislation.

The terms of the treaty were on the whole speculative, stating only the principles except for the detailed provisions on the matter of simplified transfer of bank accounts. However, there was one outstanding feature of this treaty, an article whereby Italy was bound to improve her industrial conditions on the lines of prohibition of night labor, minimum age for child labor, length of working day and compulsory weekly rest day. The conditions of industry in these two countries were by no means the same, except for the legal provision on weekly rest periods touching which the difference was comparatively slight. Italian labor legislation was behind that of France in practically every other respect so this treaty meant for Italy a considerable effort.

Three months later, Italy entered into a treaty with Switzerland which provided in part for the reciprocal treatment of the workers of either country residing in the territory of the other. The specific matter covered is in Article 17 which provides for mutual investigation into the workmen's insurance laws in operation in the other country and for the enactment of laws giving equal insurance advantages to the workers of both countries. Toward the close of the year, Italy was a partner in still another labor treaty, this time with Germany.

While certain of the more or less progressive governments were thus taking wise and measured steps forward, their rate of progress was by no means entirely satisfactory to all the advocates of labor's rights. In August, 1904, the socialist labor leaders of some of the European countries, meeting at a congress at Amsterdam proclaimed their concern and disapproval of any policy which is " merely one for amending existing society." The Congress held that "class opposition cannot be smoothed over but that on the contrary, it becomes constantly greater." The cause of the irritated controversy was Millerand's participation in the Waldeck-Rousseau Cabinet. Prior to this time the French socialists had been split into two opposing parties, one led by Jaurés who approved the ministerial action of Millerand and the other led by Guesde who disapproved the so-called "revisionist policy" or the attempt to change the well tried and successful policy of the class war.

The Amsterdam Congresss readopted the Dresden resolution, declaring that "Social democracy cannot exercise supreme power in society as at present constituted." It confirmed the socialist party's refusal to take any "responsibility for the political and economic conditions which arise out of the capitalist system of production;" it emphasized class differences. The Congress finally placed its hopes in the Social Democratic parties for practically every kind of social betterment, including labor legislation in order to "make it possible for the working class to fulfil their destiny in the political and general life of the age." [1]

The irritation of the working class over the industrial system and their philosophy had already been manifest even before the appearance of the Communist Manifesto. The resolutions adopted and opinions expressed at all of the Socialist Congresses indicate this, and, as early as 1896, the Congress of London, comtemplating an international strike for the universal liberation of the workers, took action for creating in each country a central labor union committee. The Amsterdam Congress rejected the so-called general strike but at the same time, recognizing the increase

[1] *Internationaler Sozialisten Kongress zu Amsterdam 14 bis 20 August, 1904.* Berlin, *Expedition der Buchhandlung Vorwärts*, 1904. Also W. E. Walling, *Socialism of To-day*, pp. 14-24.

of labor solidarity, declared for the further strengthening of the class organizations so as "to create the conditions necessary for the success of the mass strike on the day when the latter may be found necessary or useful." [1]

Shortly after the close of this Congress, the International Association for Legal Protection of Labor held its third Delegates' Meeting at Basel.[2] Eleven governments sent their official representatives. These with the regular delegates from various national branches, considered the questions of industrial poisons, night work of women and children, home industry, and social insurance. Committees were appointed in order to study these questions separately and exclusively. With regard to industrial poisons, lead was the chief subject considered and it was suggested by the committee in charge that the prevention of lead poisoning should be considered in connection with each industry in which this poison is used. It was further suggested by the same committee that experts be engaged to compile and publish a list of the poisonous materials used in industry grouped according to their serious effects.

The most significant thing at this conference was the position taken by the assembly in reference to the application of social insurance. It was held explicitly that a laborer had the right to the benefits of insurance and legal protection where he works, regardless of his nationality or residence. In other words, if a worker be injured in a certain factory, no matter whether he be an alien or citizen, he should be accorded equal and identical legal protection the same as any other workman, in the way of compensation for injury or incapacity. The application of such a principle to actual international agreements had already been illustrated

[1] *Ibid.*, pp. 389-390.

[2] Sept. 26-27, 1904.

by the treaties between Italy and Switerland and Italy and France on this very subject.

Within a few months,[1] the government of Italy signed still another treaty with Germany agreeing to give to the German workers in her territory the same insurance benefits that they were given in Germany. The insurance system of Germany was already a highly commended institution, dating as far back as 1883,[2] wide in its scope and efficient in its management. The task Italy assumed by this deliberate agreement with Germany was no indication of a half-hearted policy.

Treaties for mutually granting equal or equivalent insurance benefits to the workers of the contracting parties, which started in 1904, began to attract attention among the more progressive states. Thereafter international treaties of this nature were signed year by year, at least among three or four states, and affected the interests of ever-widening circles of the working population. The year 1905 began with the signing of such a treaty between Germany and Austria-Hungary, on January 19, guaranteeing in addition "reciprocity of protection of labor." This was succeeded in April by an accident insurance treaty between Belgium and Luxemburg—a treaty which laid down for the first time specific laws to be applied in both countries so as to ensure proper execution of the terms of the treaty. The reciprocal grant of compensation according to a later amendatory agreement was to be withheld only in case the worker was employed for less than half a year intermittently in transport service outside the state where the employer's concern was located.

[1] December 3, 1904. Chatelain, p. 194.

[2] *Social Insurance in Germany*, 1883-1911, Dawson; also *Workingmen's Insurance in Europe* by Frankel and Dawson, 1910.

6. *Berne Conference of 1905*

From May 8 to 17, 1905, at the invitation of the Swiss government, the first of the most important international labor conferences in history was held at Berne.[1] Since the Berlin Congress which was the first of the official international labor conferences, half a generation had to elapse before all the governments of leading industrial importance could be assembled under governmental auspices. Switzerland, as ever the champion of international labor protection was the host of the occasion.

Fifteen European states sent their representatives,[2] in order to consider two matters of industrial importance: namely, (1) the use of white phosphorus in the manufacture of matches, and (2) the employment of women during the night. The subject matter being so limited and practical and the delegates being neither mere academicians nor agitators but men of responsibility in actual governmental affairs, the result of the conference was inevitably concrete and tangible, hence its direct significance to the world of labor. From the outset, these two questions were committed to two separate groups of the conference for intensive study. Needless to say that the task of abolishing the evils, both of poison and of women's night work was one of great difficulty. The fact that Russia and Japan, then at war, were nonparticipants in the conference, added greatly to the difficulty of prohibiting the use of white phosphorus

[1] For a full account of this conference, see: (1) *Revue Économique Internationale*, 1906, vol. iv, p. 387, *et seq.*; article by E. Mahaim, entitled "La protection internationale ouvrière—les conventions de Berne et l'assemblee de Geneve." (2) Mahaim, *op. cit.*, pp. 224-291. (3) Chatelain, *op. cit.*, pp. 104-125. (4) Lowe, *op. cit.*, pp. 65-70.

[2] The U. S. was not represented; nor was Japan, though invited, on account of the war with Russia. This circumstance made this second important official conference again a "European" affair, instead of a universal international affair.

because Japan had already become a formidable competitor of Sweden, Norway, Hungary and other countries in the manufacture and sale of matches. However, a way out of this was discovered finally, through providing that in case Japan, together with the other nations present, should adhere to the convention formally by December 31, 1907, then upon fulfilment of that condition it would become universally unlawful to manufacture, import or sell matches containing white phosphorus.

The matter of prohibiting the night work of women was one bristling with difficulties. There was a wide variation in the legislative status of this matter in different countries. The minimum age of women admitted to night work was in some countries, like Belgium and Portugal, as high as twenty-one; but on the whole lower ages prevailed, that of Spain being fourteen, of Luxemburg and Hungary sixteen, *etc.* Then there were differences in the application of the laws prohibiting female night labor; some applied only where more than ten workers were employed and somewhere less were employed. Whether or not power-driven machinery was in use in the establishment made a difference in the application of the law in many countries. The task for the conference was to determine a standard of regulation as high as possible but at the same time sufficiently broad so as to be capable of general adoption. The convention as finally adopted by the conference was a draft subject to transformation into binding conventions through direct governmental negotiation.[1]

According to the draft convention on the subject of the prohibition of the use of white phosphorus, the contracting

[1] For the original terms of these two conventions translated into English, see *Report III, League of Nations. Report on the Employment of Women and Children*, prepared by the Organizing Committee for the International Labor Conference, Washington, 1919, pp. 16-19, 60-62.

parties agreed to prohibit in their respective territories the manufacture, importation and sale of matches containing the said material. Each state was to take the separate administrative measures necessary for the proper execution of the terms of the treaty. As provided in practically every convention of similar nature thenceforth concluded, it was left optional to each state to apply this convention to its colonies, possessions or protectorates. Provisions were incorporated to ensure a certain degree of permanency to the agreement. Once the declaration of adhesion to the convention was deposited with the Swiss Federal Council, it bound the depositing state to the terms of the treaty for five years, at least. Even after the lapse of five years, the denúnciation of the convention was to take effect only after a year's time from the date of notification of the denunciation.

With regard to the prohibition of women's night work, the final draft adopted by the conference gave unmistakable evidence of the noble efforts and high standards of the committee in charge. The employment of women during the night in industrial undertakings was thereby prohibited without distinction of age in all countres adhering to the convention. The most notable exception was that this should not apply to undertakings where either less than ten persons or only the members of the family were employed. It was incumbent upon the contracting states to define the term "industrial undertakings" as distinguished from commercial or agricultural. The convention definitely defined the term "night" as consisting of at least eleven consecutive hours with the hours between 10 P. M. and 5 A. M. included therein. Only in such states as had had no regulation of the night work of women theretofore was it permitted, for a maximum of three years, to have the prohibition apply to only ten night-hours instead of eleven. There were certain other exceptions providing for the cases of *force majeure* and work with materials subject to rapid deterioration in which case the convention might be suspended. For seasonal industries the reduction of night rest to ten hours for sixty days of the year was allowed. Other provisions of the convention, relating to its application to the protectorates, colonies, or possessions and its denunciation by the contracting states, were very similar to those of the convention on the use of white phosphorus except that the convention prohibiting women's night work, bound the contracting states for a twelve-year period. This convention was adhered to by eleven states: Austria, Belgium, France, Germany, Hungary, Italy, Holland, Luxemburg, Portugal, Spain, and Switzerland. The governments of Great Britian, Norway, Sweden and Denmark refused to sign. The convention on white phosphorus was signed for all these countries except the representatives of Great Britain and Norway, who because of lack of authority, were unable to sign.

The terms of these conventions are, as judged by our present notions, nothing unusual, but their importance as setting up certain standards in international labor legislation, must not be underrated. As we shall see later, they were indeed the very basis of much of the deliberation at the Washington Conference of 1919.

Shortly after the conference adjourned, the Swiss government issued [1] a circular note to the governments of Europe suggesting a diplomatic conference in order to turn the draft of the above stated conventions into conventions with binding force. The response to this note was on the whole favorable, and resulted in the actual convocation of a diplomatic assembly during the fall of the following year.

[1] June 26, 1905. See *Bulletin des internationalen Arbeitsamtes*, I (7-8), p. xxxii.

7. Subsequent events (1905-1907)

The international events which followed the Berne Conference were both gratifying and promising, with treaties signed and congresses started with ever-widening range of possibilities of labor protection.[1]

Luxemburg concluded with Germany, on September 2, an accident insurance treaty similar to the one she entered into with Belgium in April. The agreement covered railroad men and those whose place of employment was outside the state where the employers concern was located and who were employed for less than six months. Such employees in case of accident were henceforth to receive insurance benefits from the state where the accident took place.

Up to this time, we have witnessed that Italy, Germany and Luxemburg were busily engaged in making labor treaties. During the year 1906, France proved herself an initiator of a series of international agreements for labor protection. In January of this year (1906) she reopened the Franco-Italian negotiation of 1904 which had to do with simplification of transfer of bank accounts. Toward the end of thc year negotiations were consummated by the ratification of a pact, whereby a deposit amounting to 1500 francs could be transferred from one country to the other free of charge. Then in February France signed an accident insurance treaty with Belgium, which was precisely the same arrangement as the treaty signed with Luxemburg during the preceding year.[2]

Intent upon carrying out her labor-legislation program, France resumed her negotiations with Italy in June on the

[1] For full accounts of international labor treaties signed during this period see Chatelain, pp. 176-232; Lowe, pp. 93-128; Mahaim, pp. 221-308, For the reproduction of texts of important treaties affecting labor see Mahaim, *op. cit.*, pp. 311-380, annexes.

[2] *Bulletin of the International Labor Office*, I, (4-6), pp. 153-154.

subject of compensation for accidents. This was broadly referred to in the treaty of 1904, but now definite and detailed provisions were made prescribing the manner in which equality of treatment could be guaranteed to the workers of both countries. By the terms of this treaty the consular service was utilized as the necessary medium of effective and efficient execution of the mutual grant of insurance to the injured insured person.

France signed during the same month [June, 1906] still another accident insurance treaty with Luxemburg,[1] the contents of which was practically the same as of the others which preceded.

In the latter part of June, 1906, Switzerland issued a notice convoking an international diplomatic conference, after having definitely ascertained the readiness of the powers to participate. The purpose of the conference was to give final authority to the conventions drafted the previous year at Berne. The conference met at the same place from September 17th to 26th (1906), as arranged by Switzerland. Austria, Belgium, Hungary, Great Britain, France, Germany, Italy, Luxemburg, the Netherlands, Spain, Portugal, Sweden, Switzerland and Denmark signed the convention prohibiting women's night work, with the provision that Denmark should be allowed to ratify the convention after her factory law was revised in the fall of 1910. As to the convention prohibiting the use of white phosphorus in matches, only seven states—Denmark, France, Italy, Luxemburg, Germany, Switzerland and the Netherlands — signed, while others who were signatories to the draft of 1906 failed for various reasons to sign. One notable matter which occupied a large amount of the time of the conference was the creation of an international com-

[1] *Op. cit.*, II, (1), pp. 4-5.

mission, to be instituted permanently for the purpose of: (1) giving opinions on disputed points and complaints; (2) investigating and reporting facts; (3) serving as the final resort for arbitration in case request is made by one of the interested parties; and (4) considering programs for conferences on industrial questions.

This was an excellent idea and as such, *i. e.*, only as a *voeu*, it was agreed to and received signatures of representatives of ten states,[1] but the preparations were inadequate for the establishment of such an office with the broad powers proposed. The plan consequently fell through. Generally speaking, the spirit of the conference was progressive. Such alterations as were proposed and adopted in the draft conventions widened the scope and raised the standards of international labor legislation. For instance, the terms of the original draft were so changed that colonies, possessions and protectorates could adhere to the convention by mere notification by their local governments to the Swiss Federal Council. Also the clause which had made the execution of the white phosphorus agreement conditional upon the adhesion of all the states represented, including Japan, was dropped from the convention. High commendation is due to the government of Switzerland for bringing to fruition the agreements which were destined to affect the lives of millions of workers of the world.[2]

As soon as the Berne diplomatic conference closed, the fourth Delegates' Meeting of the International Association for Labor Legislation was held at Geneva from September

[1] *Cf.* Chatelain, pp. 118-119.

[2] For the widening effect of these conventions: Compare No. 4, p. 6 of *Publications de l'association internationale pour la protection légale des travailleurs*, with No. 8, *Publications of International Labor Office and Report III* of the Organizing Committee for Washington Conference, 1919, pp. 62-65, 20-22.

27 to 29 (1904). During the two-year period intervening between this and the last conference of this association, national sections had been established in Great Britain (1904), United States (1906), Denmark (1906), and Spain (1906). Thus the conference this time was represented by twelve national branches and had eighty-two delegates. The agenda of the conference consisted of: (1) child labor; (2) industrial poisons; (3) night work for young persons; (4) maximum working day; (5) home industry; and (6) insurance. The resolutions adopted by the various committees of the conference which considered these topics separately and exclusively proposed admirable standards within practical limits.

The time had evidently now arrived when the interests of the general public were sufficiently alive to the needs and possibilities of international coöperation for labor protection. Hardly a day had elapsed after the close of the assembly of the International Association at Geneva before an international congress was opened at Milan to consider the problem of unemployment. This was the first international assembly convoked to discuss this gravely important matter. The congress was held October 1-2 (1906). It did not attempt to eliminate the causes of unemployment by suggesting a radical program of reformation but it undertook to formulate methods for meeting and combating its evils. Inevitably the hours of work, wages, contracts of labor, better adjustment of opportunities for labor, and above all, state control or regulation of employment were considered points of approach to the root of the problem. The congress passed resolutions on matters of immediate significance to the protective labor movement. It suggested among other things the establishment of free public employment offices, government subsidy to the employment agencies established by the workers, and the establishment, finally, of an international employment bureau.

Toward the end of October, of this same year, two other international conferences affecting labor were held in Italy, one at Pavia and the other at Milan, one closely succeeding the other.[1] The Pavia conference was one of the periodic congresses on rice cultivation where the idea was proposed of a joint council with representatives of both capital and labor for conciliatory purposes. The conference at Milan was also one of the periodic international conferences on the weekly day of rest. The proceedings of the conference and its resolutions show that it was far from being mere propaganda advocating more rest and ease for the worker. The conference proceeded judicially and scientifically to devise practical plans for granting to all workers of every branch of industry, commerce, and trade the necessary weekly rest-day.

With the progress of the times, the labor treaties signed by the advanced states became increasingly better adapted to actual needs. The treaty which Germany entered into with the Netherlands on August 27, 1907, furnishes an instance of a treaty based on careful study of the conditions of its application. It was an accident-insurance treaty like the German-Luxemburg Treaty, aiming at equality of insurance benefits but stipulating in particular the compulsory features of insurance and minor details, such as the treatment of the employees on transportation lines.

Nevertheless, enthusiasm over the national or governmental programs of labor protection of this period receives at times a chilling blast from occasional acts which reveal the dubious motives on the part of some of the governments in proposing paternalistic reform-legislation. When the powers met at the Hague during August, 1907, for the second International Peace Conference, they were too interested in the national honor and sovereignty of each

[1] *Bulletin of the International Law Office,* I (9-12), pp. 604-605.

nation to give heed to the proposal of submitting to arbitration any international labor disputes. Here the proposition was made by the Portuguese representative that an article of the Hague Conventions should be replaced with a new article providing in part that international disputes including the interpretaton or application of labor agreements should finally be subject to compulsory arbitration. The governments were too jealous of their national honor to yield to an international tribunal of justice, even though it seemed to be for the interest ultimately of labor.[1]

8. *Socialist Congresses at Stuttgart and Copenhagen and the intervening events (1908-1913)*

Such a circumstance as is described above seemed to furnish ample justification for the kind of expressions used time and again at the International Socialist Labor Congresses. The congress which met in 1907 at Stuttgart with representatives of all the socialist parties of the world (except the French) present, reaffirmed their program of class struggle for the "complete enfranchisement of the proletariat from the bonds of intellectual, political and economic serfdom."

It should be borne in mind that the philosophy of the socialist internationals, at least since the Zurich Congress of 1893, was no longer the vain speculation of agitators who styled themselves "socialist thinkers." Since the Zurich Congress of the Internationale, where they decided to admit, by a vote of 16 national parties against 2, "all labor unions recognizing the need of working-class organization and political action," this organization had ceased to be purely socialistic. The membership of labor unions within the congress increased year after year.

[1] See *Bulletin of the International Labor Office*, II (3), p. 428—the case is cited in full by Lowe, pp. 55-56.

To the Stuttgart Congress of 1907, the British Labor Party, which explicitly declared itself to be *non-socialist,* was admitted, and it had five out of ten votes allotted to British political organizations. Altogether at this congress the British trade unions had fifteen out of twenty votes allotted to Great Britain. The congress recognized definitely that " there is an ever-widening domain in the proletarian struggle of the classes in which they can only reap advantages by concerted action and by coöperation " between the socialist party and labor organizations. Here labor and socialism united and they declared it their "duty to render mutual support " for the emancipation of the proletariat.[1] The situation was growing tense.

The International Association for Labor Legislation held its fifth general assembly at Lucerne, September 28-30, 1908. The matters taken up for discussion were numerous. They were largely the continuation of the problems considered previously, namely, the prohibition of night work of young persons, the limiting of working hours of women, *etc.* That this was not merely discursive was seen later, as the principles laid down here were embodied in the Berne Convention of 1913. The recommendation and definition made here as to an eight-hour shift for workers in coal mines were also found a valuable prototype of labor legislation. Mention should be made in passing of the fact that the association by this time had already acquired prestige and influence, sufficient to command governmental recognition. The United States, Austria, Belgium, Denmark, France, Germany, Prussia, Saxony, Baden, Hungary, Italy, Luxemburg, The Netherlands, Norway, Sweden, Switzerland, and even the Holy See sent their official representatives to this Lucerne Conference of 1908.

[1] W. E. Walling, *op. cit.*, pp. 373-375; also *Proposals and drafts of Resolutions submitted to the International Socialist Congress of Stuttgart*, pp. 411-427.

During the year 1909 two accident insurance treaties were entered upon, one by England and France (July 3, 1909) [1] and the other by Hungary and Italy (September 19, 1909).[2]

A conference of distinctive color which met this year was the International Congress of Women, which was held at Toronto, Canada. This Congress had held its first meeting in London in 1899. The second one was held at the invitation of the National Council of Women of Canada. The activity of women in the fields of politics and labor, as we shall soon realize, was beginning to show itself an important factor in molding human destinies.

In August, 1909, one of the biennial conferences of the International Federation of Trades Union, which was first organized in 1898, was held in Paris. Samuel Gompers had been directed by the 1908 convention of the American Federation of Labor to attend this Conference, and thus American labor was for the first time brought into touch with the International Secretariat. The American Federation of Labor became affiliated with the International Federation in 1909.

The year which followed (1910) witnessed two congresses and a treaty of international significance: the Socialist Congress held at Copenhagen, the sixth general assembly of the International Association at Lugano, and the negotiations between France and Italy on labor matters. The fact that the tense industrial situation was being felt more and more keenly was evidenced by the resolutions adopted by both of these congresses, differing considerably in their mode of thinking and program of action and yet facing the same grave problems, foremost among which was unemployment.

[1] *Bulletin of Int. Lab. Office*, IV (3), pp. 163-164.

[2] *Ibid.*, V (1), pp. 1-3.

The Lugano Conference of the International Association for Labor Legislation declared itself in need of coöperation with the International Association on Unemployment. The Copenhagen Congress of the Socialist Internationale demanded "the institution by public authorities under the administration of working-class organizations, of general compulsory insurance against unemployment, the expense of which should be borne by the owners of the means of production." The Congress further declared that "unemployment is inseparable from the capitalistic mode of production and will disappear only when capitalism disappears." As "palliative measures" which alone could be hoped for under capitalism, the congress demanded among other things the collection of unemployment statistics, adoption of union-wages, increased subsidy to union funds for unemployment insurance in case of industrial crises, and laws for regulation and reduction of hours.[1]

At the Lugano Conference the topics discussed included practically every important aspect of the labor problem. Besides the problem of unemployment, this conference considered those of maximum hours of work per day, child labor, social insurance as applied to foreigners, administration of labor laws, industrial poisons and the like. One resolution which the conference adopted was of special importance. This was on the creation of wage boards for home work. The original draft of the international agreement prohibiting the employment of young persons in industry, which was finally concluded at Berne in 1913, took its definite shape at this conference. The conference also appointed a commission to prepare a report on child-labor laws in various countries.

On the prohibition of the use of lead paint and colors in

[1] *Internationaler Sozialisten Kongress zu Kopenhagen*, 28 August bis 3 September, 1910, p. 12. For details see pp. 1-113.

interior work, a suggestion was made that all commercial goods containing lead should be required to have a plain mark on it "poisonous—containing lead." The matter of "occupational diseases" again received full consideration and the conference called the attention of the Swiss Federal Council to the standards set on this subject by the conference.

We have seen in previous sections of this chapter the close relationship between Italy and France touching labor legislation. Since the conclusion of the treaty of 1904 these countries have been actively interested in the improvement of their international labor legislation. During the year 1910 (June 15) their negotiations came to partial fruition, a new agreement being made for the mutual protection of young persons employed in industry. Generally speaking, the age of protection was set at 15, but on account of the legal status in France where children above 12 could be admitted to work, it was provided in the agreement that those above 12 might be employed. The conditions for this were that those children should have completed the elementary-school education and that the consent of their protector prescribed in legal form together with their picture had been presented to the consul of their own country located in the state where the children sought employment. The contracting parties were bound to the terms for five years. Unless the denunciation of either party took place within six months before the expiration of the term, the provisions were to remain effective for another period of five years. On August 9 of the same year these two countries concluded still another agreement and established a system whereby the workers of either country, residing in the territory of the other, could be granted pension-benefits as if they had remained in their own country.

Among the international congresses held during the year

1910, those of interest to labor were one on occupational diseases held at Brussels and one on School Hygiene held in Paris. The latter was the third of the series of International Congresses on School Hygiene,—which held its first meeting of organization at Nuremberg in 1904, the second in London in 1907, the third in Paris and the fourth in Buffalo in 1913.[1] The International Prison Commission, which has a history of more than a generation dating as far back as the London conference of 1872, held its eighth general assembly in Washington, D. C., in 1910.

Of a number of treaties concluded during 1911, those with direct bearing upon the interests of labor were comparatively few. Germany and Sweden in concluding their Commerce and Navigation Treaty on May 2, *did* look toward the insurance of labor in a measure similar to that prescribed by the German-Italian accident insurance treaty, but little was accomplished in practice.

By far the most important treaty in the history of international labor legislation was signed on August 9, 1911, between France and Denmark.[2] For the first time the nations willingly entered into an agreement which involved in a certain sense the surrendering of their national pride for the sake of the higher justice that might be rendered upon an international basis. The treaty specified four classes of questions which had ultimately to be submitted to the verdict of the Hague Tribunal and international protection of workers became thereby a subject of compulsory arbitration. "The interpretation and application of the stipulations of the convention relating to trade and navigation, sanitary questions, white-slave trade," *etc.*, were brought into the same category. Although the judicial

[1] See report by J. W. Scherewsky, U. S. Public Health Service Report 144. Washington, Gov. Ptg. Office, 1913.

[2] *Bulletin of the International Labor Office*, VI (3), p. 229-230.

authority of the state rather than of the Hague was the primary agency to decide the cases of dispute and the Hague Tribunal had no power of annulling the decision of a state judiciary, if no compromise could be reached between the states, the Hague Tribunal was automatically authorized to arbitrate after a year had elapsed from the date of notification by one of the parties.

Toward the close of the year 1911, two private sickness-insurance establishments (one of Sweden,—General Association of Sick Funds; the other,—Danish United Central Association of Sick Funds) were negotiating to the end that in case a member of the sick fund of one country removed to the other, the transfer of his membership to the sick fund of the country to which he removed could be made exempt from entrance fee, regardless of age, health conditions, *etc.* The only exception to this was that people joining the fund at an age above forty could not transfer their membership. This improvement, together with the detailed plans for settling disputes which were proposed by these two concerns, furnish us an excellent example of international coöperation.

During the year 1911 the International Federation of Trades Union Congress was held in Budapest under the International Secretariat. James Duncan, first vice-president of the A. F. of L. was the American delegate. The Zurich Congress of the International Federation of Trades Union in 1913 was attended by Perkins, the president of the Cigarmakers International Union.

Parallel with the advance of the protective labor movement, the International Association for Labor Legislation increased its activities. The association met for its seventh general assembly of delegates at Zurich from September 10 to 12 in 1912. The association with its highly increased membership and well-merited recognition was an effective organ to stimulate progressive labor legislation in various countries. It sent messages of "thanks," as they called them, which were nothing short of "encouragements," to the governments of the United States, Switzerland, Spain, Hungary, New Zealand, South Africa, *etc.*, for such action as the prohibition of night work of women or prohibition of import of matches containing white phosphorus. The resolutions adopted and actions taken by the conference indicate that this association had long ceased to be an organization for mere expression of principles. The discussions dealt with highly specialized and increasingly more technical or specific problems. The discussion on industrial hygiene, the protection of railroad workers, dock employees, miners, tunnel constructors, quarrymen, *etc.*, the problems of home workers and the methods of administration of wage boards, international statistics of morbidity and mortality of workers and the like — all pointed to the higher scientific standards of the association. We will waive their description, however, for the sake of the more general trend of the times which we aim to trace. During the month of July, 1912, Germany signed two accident insurance treaties, one with Belgium and the other with Italy.[1] The latter particularly was far more precise and comprehensive than any treaty of a similar kind which preceded. It included not simply accident insurance which guaranteed equality of compensation to the foreign worker in case of injury, but it covered the cases of invalidity, old age and the death of the wage-earner. Much can be learned from a study of the stipulations of this treaty for the practical application of international insurance agreements under differing conditions, but we must dismiss the matter with only this passing mention.

[1] *Op. cit.*, VIII (2) also (3-4).

9. *Berne Conference of 1913* [1]

The last of all the important international labor conferences prior to the war was officially convoked by the Swiss Government and met at Berne from September 15 to 25, 1913. The delegates to the Lugano Conference of the International Association, who sent words of congratulation and appreciation to the Swiss Federal Council for taking steps for this conference, were largely responsible for the convocation and achievements of the conference. Nineteen European states were invited, but five of lesser importance failed to attend. The delegates represented were from Austria, Hungary, Germany, Belgium, Denmark, Spain, Great Britain, France, Italy, Norway, the Netherlands, Portugal, Sweden and Russia.

Before the Swiss Government entered into official communication with the other powers, the International Labor Office had set itself to the task of making drafts and a program which would serve as a basis for the conference. The memoranda previously submitted by the International Labor Office incorporated the results of painstaking study and extensive expert information. There was acute political tension in the air but the delegates proceeded calmly with their program. The program was limited to two subjects or drafts of international agreements: (1) prohibition of the industrial night-work of persons under sixteen; (2) establishment of a maximum working-day of ten hours for women and young persons. Thus, as in the case of the Berne Conference of 1905, the objects put forward here were concrete and limited and the conference failed of immediate effect only because the outbreak of the war prevented a meeting of the diplomatic conference for official ratification of the draft conventions which it adopted.

[1] For documentary sources on this conference see the *Bulletin of the Int. Lab. Office* vol. viii, the numbers for the year 1913. For concise account see Love, *op. cit.*, pp. 87-92.

The draft-conventions finally adopted by the conference [1] were more specific in detail than the draft originally submitted by the International Association. However, the principles embodied in the original were retained with one notable exception,—the lowering of the age-limit from 18 to 16. Below 14 years of age the prohibition was made absolute. As in the case of the Berne Convention of 1906, the present convention applied only to industrial undertakings employing more than 10 persons. Nor did it apply to undertakings where only members of the family are engaged. The term "night" was defined as 11 consecutive hours, including the hours between 10 p. m. and 5 a. m. For workers emlpoyed in baking, the period from 9 p. m. to 4 a. m. might be substituted for that from 10 p. m. to 5 a. m. An exception in regard to a rest period was allowed in coal and lignite mines, provided that the hours between two work-periods were more than thirteen. Workers above 14 years of age could be employed in the night if the state or public interest demanded it or in case of emergency. For female workers, 16 years was set as the legal age below which all the restrictions of both this and the convention of 1906 should apply. Special consideration was given to the climatic and racial differences in colonies, possessions, and protectorates. In such places and in extra-European states, the period of uninterrupted rest could be shortened to less hours than 11, provided that total rest periods were equivalent to 11 hours. Finally, ten years of delay before the execution of the convention were allowed in the case of workers above 14 in certain undertakings such as melting, annealing and refining of glass, and the work directly connected with furnaces in steel and iron production.

Had the war not prevented, the convention would have

[1] See *Bulletin of the International Labor Office*, series for 1913.

taken effect after two years from the time of the deposit of the ratification by all the countries. The countries which gave their signatures to this draft convention were Austria, Hungary, Belgium, France, Germany, Great Britain, Italy, Holland, Norway, Portugal, Sweden and Switzerland.

The other draft convention limited the working hours of women and children under 16. Ten hours was set as the standard. But half an hour's work could be allowed per day as a maximum, so long as the total of sixty hours per week was not overstepped. For work continuing more than six hours, a rest period must be given, once at least, after six hours of work. Other provisions were the exception allowed in case emergency or public interest demanded it, for work with materials subject to rapid deterioration, for seasonal industry, *etc.* One hundred and eighty hours per year was set as the maximum over-time allowance. From two to seven years of delay was allowed in the case of certain industries, the readjustment of which in a shorter period was deemed impracticable by the conference.

This draft convention received the signatures of the same nations as the first, but the diplomatic conference which had been contemplated for their formal ratification could not be called on account of the war. The Swiss Government, after having faithfully issued several notes on this matter to the governments concerned, finally gave up hope and communicated to the powers the suggestion that " the conference be postponed to some future date."

CHAPTER IV

The World War, The Peace Conference and the Labor Charter

1. *The outbreak of the war; the attitude of the socialist and labor parties*

A concerted attack on protective labor legislation was ushered in by the outbreak of the war. In every country without exception reckless attempts were made to tear down the bulwark of statutory protection of labor in the name of the most catastrophic war in human history. The protection and privileges which years of struggle had secured for labor were set aside for the manufacture of munitions. Even in England the former standards of labor regarding age limits, sex distinctions, length of hours, safety, wage negotations and everything except perhaps the money wage paid, were either lowered or abrogated.[1] Money wages rose abnormally, but this only further complicated the situation.

The havoc wrought on the plea of emergency did not cease until the United States began to participate actively in the world conflict. Even in the United States there were in the beginning attempts to break down the legal safeguards of labor.[2] Thus the war which involved all the civilized peoples of the world was a blow to all the progressive pro-

[1] See *Bulletin of U. S. Bureau of Labor Statistics*, no. 221, "Hours, fatigue and health in British munition factories;" no. 223, "Employment of women and juveniles during the war;" no. 236, "Industrial efficiency and fatigue," *etc.*

[2] The state legislatures of Connecticut, Massachusetts, New Hampshire, Vermont, *etc.*, enacted statutes authorizing suspension of labor laws. The New Hampshire law prohibited strikes.

grams of labor legislation. The war automatically brought to a standstill of plans for international conferences scores of which but for it would have been held. The International Federation of Trades Union had arranged to meet in San Francisco in 1915 on the occasion of the World's Fair. The Congress was to meet simultaneously with the Convention of the A. F. of L. But the plan fell through. The Socialist Internationale which had held its last gathering, a special peace congress, at Basel in 1912, would have met in Vienna on August 23, 1914, just fifty years from the birth of the first Internationale. The place of the congress was thereafter transferred to Paris and the date changed to August 9, but the holding of an international gathering of this nature was found entirely out of the question and was given up. The work of the International Socialist Bureau, which had for years operated actively with Camille Huysmans as secretary and Emile Vandervelde as chairman, was also abandoned with the entry of Vandervelde into the war cabinet of Belgium. That an exponent of internationalism like this veteran socialist should have voluntarily accepted membership in the ministry of war was indicative of the sinister situation from the point of view of socialists. The seat of the International Socialist Bureau was transferred from Brussels to the Hague, and placed under the supervision of the neutral Dutch Socialists.

The invasion of Belgium by Germany which marked the darkest pages in the history of the Great War afforded incidentally a crucial test of the strength of international socialism.[1] There was a large percentage of socialists among

[1] See an enlightening treatise on this matter by Morris Hillquit, *Yale Review*, Oct., 1915, pp. 39-49. "Socialism and Internationalism." For a comprehensive survey of the attitude of the socialist and labor parties in all countries toward the war, see pt. iv, *American Labor Year Book 1916*; pts. i and v in volumes for *1917-18* and *1919-20*; also "The Socialists and the War" by W. E. Walling.

the troops which fought on both sides in the fierce battle on the Belgian frontier. It is noteworthy that the labor element in all countries seemed to take a definite stand on the war. The Belgian Labor Party had already abandoned all anti-war demonstrations. The Council of the Party after deliberation issued on August 3, 1914, a manifesto to all socialist workers justifying the war as "self-defense." The invasion was regarded as an act of "militarist barbarism" and "fatality of events." And thus the war on their side was regarded as a war for the "cause of democracy and of political liberty in Europe." The Council instructed the socialist members of the legislative chamber to vote for the war budgets.

On the other hand, in Germany, the side of the aggressors, it was also the case that a large majority of the socialists supported the war. When the first war budget was presented to the Reichstag at the outbreak of the war, only 14 of the 110 Socialist members voted against it.[1] In the course of time the opposition did increase so that as many as thirty members left the Reichstag and when the war-loan measure of December 15, 1915, was introduced, twenty opposition votes were cast by the party members.

In France an unexpected phenomenon was witnessed. The labor and socialist elements came into close harmony and concertedly supported the war. Radical and class conscious syndicalist-labor stood for the war. As soon as war was declared by Germany, Jules Guésde and Marcel Sembat who had long been strongly opposed to socialist ministerialism, immediately became members of the French cabinet with the approval of the party. Later Albert Thomas also came in as Minister of Munitions.

[1] It is of interest to note in passing that among those who opposed the war budget were Liebknecht, Hasse, Klara Zetkin, Rosa Luxemburg, Kautsky and Mehring, some of whom later led the Spartacan revolution.

In England the British Labor Party which is a federation of trade unions and socialist organizations showed an unswerving pro-war attitude from the very outset. Despite its constitutional provision whereby all the constituents of the party and their representatives were pledged for "uncompromising independence from other political parties," the Labor Party itself willingly joined with the other parties. Three labor members of the Party joined the coalition government which was formed in May, 1915. Some served in the war cabinet and one even became a "government whip." The 1916 convention of the Party, held in January, voted their approval of the entry of those members into the government. Even after the downfall of the Asquith government, in December, 1916, when Lloyd George offered certain seats of the government, about to be formed, to the labor members, the party accepted the offer. This resulted in having as many as seven labor members in the cabinet, one of whom sat with the Inner Council of Five. The participation of the labor element in the war-cabinet became a matter of such exuberant enthusiasm that in the course of time the action of the labor members began to seem a surrender of labor's rights rather than the support of the war in the interests of labor. The munition act which deprived the laborer of his right to strike was introduced by the cabinet with the labor members sitting therein. The act deprived the worker not only of his right to strike but even of his freedom to quit his job without the consent of the court. Severe penal servitude was imposed for violations. Military conscription was heartily supported by the labor men. This involved industrial compulsion which in substance and in consequence smashed the interests of labor to pieces. Philip Snowden, the labor member of Parliament, speaking of the position of these labor men in the cabinet said that it "will be one which nobody will envy," and that they had "disrupted the political labor movement probably beyond the possibility of repair." [1]

Another writer, commenting on the same situation says, "The war caught British labor unprepared. It required three years for the workers to find themselves and begin to shape a policy. So it is with the coming of peace. The post-war world demanded a policy and labor was unready. If there had been a determined program backed by five million convinced workers, it would have won its way against Governments, Parliaments *etc.*" [2]

What the attitude or even the sentiment of socialist labor parties of Hungary was could not be definitely ascertained because there was no representation of their parties in the Reichstag. There was, moreover, a strict censorship which suppressed all liberal or anti-administration propaganda. In the Austrian Empire, on the contrary, the stand of the Austrian Social Democracy was clean-cut and decidedly pro-war. Austria before the war had already attained high industrial development in certain quarters. The labor movement had proportionately been active through a history of half a century or more. Since 1901 labor had representation in the Austrian parliament, electing as many as ten members. In the Social Democracy of Austria there were two dominant groups; one German, with some 1,370 branches and 146,000 members and the other Bohemian with 2,480 branches and 144,000 members before the war. On March 25-28, 1916, a national conference of the German-Austrian Socialist party was held in Vienna. This party with its five daily, eleven weekly and thirteen other newspapers and periodicals of far-reaching influence, passed a resolution upholding the national war policies as "justifiable."

[1] *Am. Lab. Yr. Book*, 1917-18, p. 23. Article by P. Snowden.

[2] Arthur Gleason in *The Socialist Review*, December, 1919, p. 8.

How emphatically the American Federation of Labor voiced its pro-war sentiment is a well known fact, and it is hardly necessary to mention the hearty support which American labor gave to the government of the United States when she assumed active part in the conflict.[1] There was some opposition in the United States from socialists and radical laborers but the attitude of organized labor on the whole was dictated by a strong and unqualified pro-war feeling.

Among the more important countries which participated in the world conflict, the socialists of Italy and Russia were the notable exceptions, in that they were " practically unanimous in opposing all intervention and participation " from the very outset. The Italian socialists specially opposed not only the war but the French and English parties for recklessly supporting the war, and it was they who were most active in the bringing about of the reunion of all international socialist forces. Finally it was they who made the first Zimmerwald Conference a substantial success.

In Spain and other countries, which were neutral in the beginning, the attitude of labor was also that of dubious contemplation, as it were, but the active participation of labor in the French, British and Belgian cabinets, not to mention the war-like attitude of the German socialists, had a great influence upon labor in other countries.[2]

2. *The war-time labor conditions*

The standards of labor were gradually breaking down with the temporary suspension of legal restraints. The in-

[1] See "Labor and the War: A. F. of L. and the Labor Movements of Europe and America."

[2] For an admirable historical presentation of socialism at the outbreak of the war see *Socialism in Thought and Action* by H. Laidler, pp. 267-282, published by Macmillan, 1920.

stance which is cited below is sufficient to illustrate the awful extent of the breakdown. It was discovered by an English official inquiry that "in a certain munition factory the prolonging of the hours of work had increased the number of the cases of sickness to such an extent that in four weeks (in May, 1919) only 53%, in two other weeks 59.6%, of the lost time could be made up by overtime work. Both employers and foremen broke down under strain." [1]

The memoranda issued by the British Health of Munition Workers Committee during war-time contain information depicting the serious conditions of labor as affected by the war, as well as the wise steps which were taken by the government in order to ameliorate those conditions. The Committee was appointed in the middle of September, 1915, by the Minister of Munitions, "to consider and advise on questions of industrial fatigue, hours of labor and other matters affecting the personal health and physical efficiency of workers in munition factories and workshops." The committee, twelve in number, consisted of interested members of Parliament, representatives of the factory department, experts on matters of industrial hygiene, *etc.* The committee investigated various industrial centers, took evidence from the employers' and workers' representatives, visited a large number of factories and workshops, and finally submitted a report with recommendations to the government. Its findings are on various aspects of wartime labor, such as the continuation of Sunday work, prolonged hours of labor, fatigue, sickness, accidents, general breakdown of health, *etc.* On the question of overtime work, for instance, the committee admitted that "it must continue," but at the same time it recommended that the

[1] *British Ministry of Munitions, Interim report on Industrial Efficiency and Fatigue* (1917), Cd. 8511, p. 44, cited in *U. S. Bureau of Labor Statistics*, bulletin no. 254, pp. 5-6.

average weekly-hours should not exceed 65 to 67, including overtime. Except for "sudden and unexpected circumstances" hours in excess of 65 should only be worked for "short periods." "Wherever practicable," the committee further suggested, "the overtime should be concentrated within three or four days in the week." The committee "wished to discourage" Sunday work. With regard to night work, it pointed out that work continued through the night was "uneconomical" and that "though wages are paid at a higher rate, more particularly during the last two or three hours of the twelve-hour shift [the output] is generally lower." [1]

The vast increase of women employed in factories and munition plants was an inevitable evil. In the spring of 1916, over half a million women were added to the laboring force of Great Britain. In July, 1914, the number of women workers was 5,020,000, but in April, 1916, it had increased to 5,490,000. The rate of increase during the 21 months of war as compared with peace times was five to one.[2]

The unavoidable evil effects of the employment of women under such conditions do not need statistical proof. They were manifested, to use the words of the committee's report, in "disturbances of digestion, due to unsuitable food, irregular and hurried meals or fatigue; anemia with possibly associated disease of the heart and circulatory system; headache; nervous exhaustion; muscular pain and weakness; flat foot and derangement of special physiological functions."

Fatigue was found to exist not only among women but

[1] Memoranda Nos. 1 and 5 of the Committee; for a summary of the Committee's conclusions, see *U. S. Bureau of Labor Statistics Bulletin*, no. 221, pp. 8-13.

[2] See the table in *U. S. Bur. of Lab. Stat. Bulletin*, no. 223, p. 17.

among men and boys as well. "A dry skin, a vacant expression, and a skin rash" . . . such were only symptoms showing the tendency. On the whole they were found to be "so dull, so spiritless, so dead in look, so woebegone, and attacked with weariness to a dulling of their spirits, as to compel attention." "Lassitude, exhaustion and impaired vitality" were a common matter for all workers and the strain of war was no less tense in either France or Italy than in England. We can imagine the conditions prevailing in the rest of the belligerent nations.[1]

In France women workers were on the increase even before the war accelerated the tendency. In the chemical industries which had employed 13,085 women out of 66,768 workers before the war, there were 18,439 women out of 77,118 workers in July, 1918. In the metal industry the increase was still more startling. The pre-war figure of women workers engaged in the metal works was 17,731 out of the total of 316,071, but in January, 1918, the figure rose to 132,012 out of the total of 514,113. In the summer of 1917 an estimate was made that the increase of women workers since the outbreak of the war was 93%.[2]

The entry of the United States into the war threatened to break down the legal restraints on labor exploitation. However, the experience of Europe served as a warning. On March 4, 1917, which was more than a month before a state of war with Germany was declared, a statute was enacted whereby the President of the United States was authorized to suspend in case of national emergency the eight-hour law on government contracts provided "time and one-half" be paid to the workers for overtime.

[1] *Op. cit.*, pp. 64, 84, 85, 98, 99, 111, 115, *etc.* For full accounts of the war time labor conditions in England, see *Bulletins 221, 223* and 230 of the *U. S. Bureau of Labor Statistics.* Also *British Labor Conditions and Legislation During the War*, by Holland, published in 1920.

[2] G. Duchene in *Am. Lab. Yr. Bk.*, 1920, pp. 11-17.

On the next day a bill was introduced in the New York State Legislature providing that the law limiting the hours of work of women and children to nine a day and fifty-four a week should be suspended in the case of workers above 16 years of age or of those " engaged in the manufacture of supplies of any sort for the military and naval forces of the United States or any state." A protest was made by the New York Consumers' League and other labor organizations, but the New York Association of Employing Printers and other manufacturers' and employers' associations gave their full support to the measure.

On April 12, in the states of Vermont and New Hampshire laws were enacted, the former allowing the suspension of laws limiting the working hours of women and children for the duration of the war, and the latter prohibiting strikes or lockouts in factories or munition plants engaged in military or naval service.

On April 20, three labor bills prepared by the Senate Special War Committee were introduced in the New York State Assembly. The first bill provided " for the suspension by the industrial commission, after investigation, for the period of the war and two months thereafter, of any provision of the labor law." The second was " for relieving children, aged twelve or more, from school attendance between April 1 and November 1, during the war for agricultural work," and the third was " for suspension by the public service commission during the war of the railroad full-crew law for the period of the war."

Briefly, such was the tenor of the reactionary measures proposed in the United States [1] at the beginning of her

[1] See Solon DeLeon's "Labor Laws in War Time," a full list of laws affecting labor, proposed or enacted during the war, in *American Lab. Yr. Bk.*, vol. ii, pp. 16-21; also vol. iii, pp. 76-79; see also *Labor Laws in War Time* published by American Ass'n for Lab. Legislation, April 16, 1917.

participation in the war. But it is also noteworthy that as soon as she entered the war, that is, on the first day after she began hostilities with Germany, the Council of National Defense gave its approval to the resolution submitted by the advisory labor commission that "legislatures of the states, as well as all administrative agencies, charged with the enforcement of labor and health laws," should be urged "rigorously to maintain the existing safeguards as to the health and the welfare of the workers." A feature which was somewhat sinister in the resolution was that it at the same time urged the legislatures to delegate their powers before they adjourned to the governors of their respective states enabling the latter "to suspend or modify restrictions contained in their labor laws." New Hampshire quickly responded, and on April 16 the State Assembly authorized the governor to suspend the labor laws during the war.

A considerable amount of study has already been given to the subject of the effect of war on labor standards.[1] For our purposes it suffices simply to indicate the serious consequences which must ensue when there is a lack of international coöperation and mutual understanding. The war-time state of mind is a menace even in highly industrialized, progressive countries, undermining the security of the workers and wrecking the standards of labor legislation.

3. *International Conferences during the war — at Copenhagen, London, Vienna, the Hague, Zimmerwald, Kiental, Leeds, Stockholm and London*

The Great War spread like a conflagration. Former sponsors of labor's interests were transformed into bellicose nationalists. The Swiss and the American socialist and

[1] See a number of articles by various research investigators in pt. i of vols. ii and iii of *Am. Lab. Yr. Bk.*

labor groups issued appeals urging the meeting of an International Socialist and Labor Congress soon after the war broke out. These appeals failed; but the socialists of the neutral countries, including Norway, Sweden, Denmark and Holland, met at Copenhagen in January, 1915, and then a month thereafter (February 14, 1915) the first of the Interallied Socialist and Labor Conferences was held in London.[1] England, Belgium, France and Russia were represented. Then in April, from the 12th to the 13th, the socialists of the central empires held a meeting in Vienna. These conferences invariably denounced the war as a war of capitalism. They demanded a peace on the basis of international arbitration, disarmament, democratic control of the states or self-determination, and so forth.

The progressive women of different nations also projected and held an International Women's Conference at the Hague, in April, in order to consider "what could be done internationally even during the war for the establishment of permanent peace in the future, the repressing of hatred and revenge and the promotion of mutual understanding between the nations." The resolutions adopted by the conference could be summed up as the stand "for the principles of a just peace, for the settling of international disputes by other means than war, and the claim that women should have a voice in the affairs of the nations." What practical influence this gathering of women had on the final peace making at Paris could be seen in the letter written by President Wilson to Jane Addams who presided at the conference.[2]

The first of the war-time international conferences, in

[1] For the declaration of this conference, see *Labor's War Aims*, special bulletin of International Conciliation, June, 1918, pp. 179-181.

[2] See "Toward Peace and Freedom," organ of the Women's International League, August, 1919, p. 6.

the sense of including all nations participating in the conflict, was held at Zimmerwald, Switzerland, in September, 1915. The passports for the delegates from the Independent Labor Party and the British Socialist Party of England were withheld by their government but the delegates from France, Italy, Bulgaria, Holland, Rumania, Poland, Sweden, Norway, Denmark and the German Empire succeeded in assembling on time. The conference aimed at "common working-class action in behalf of peace." This is known as the Zimmerwald Conference. In April, 1916, another meeting was held at Kiental, Switzerland, this being the second war-time international socialist and labor conference. Italy, Sweden, Russia and Germany were represented. The tone of this conference was revolutionary. The manifesto issued with the signatures of Lenin of Russia, Bouderon of France and Ledebour of the German Reichstag, called for revolution within their respective countries. It urged refusal to support the war, immediate peace, and class war against all forms of national oppression. Up to this time the participants of these conferences had their headquarters at Berne, where the commission in charge was making plans for the continuation of the conference activities.[1]

Shortly after the outbreak of the war, the American Federation of Labor passed a resolution at its session in 1914, proposing the convocation of "an international labor conference with the representatives of organized labor of the different countries, to meet at the same time and place of the peace congress." The Executive Council of the Federation, under the authorization of the convention, then sent copies of the resolution to the International Federation of Trades Union as well as to the national trade unions in

[1] See H. Laidler, *op. cit.*, p. 285, *et seq.*

various countries.[1] This proposal was indorsed by the Canadian Trades Union Congress and the French Confédération Générale du Travail, but the other allied labor groups preferred an interallied instead of an international meeting. The British Trades Union Congress disapproved this proposal by a vote of 2 to 1, but within a year the Party reversed its decision and requested the British War Cabinet to give them permission to join in such a conference. The British Labor Party took the same steps in applying for permission. On May 1, 1916, this proposal was brought up for the consideration of the Allied Supreme Council and resulted in the formation of a commission to prepare for an international labor conference which was arranged to meet later at Leeds, England. The commission consisted of the labor leaders of Great Britain, France, Italy and Belgium. Léon Jouhaux, the secretary-general of the Confédération Générale du Travail, was appointed chairman.

The important feature of the Leeds Conference which met in July, 1916, was the resolution which was adopted and circulated not only among the allies but also the central powers. It was declared in the resolution that the peace terms which conclude the war must not only insure political and economic independence to the nations but also to the workers a "minimum of guarantees of a moral as well as of a material kind, concerning the right of coalition, emigration, social insurance, hours of labor, hygiene, and protection of labor in order to secure them against the attacks of international capitalistic competition."

The resolution urged further the creation of an international commission for the supervision of legislation on

[1] See "Labor and the War: A. F. of L. and the Labor Movements of Europe and Latin America," pp. 9-10. The resolution cited in full in "League of Nations," vol. ii, no. 5, pp. 275-276. See also *Annals of Am. Acad. of P. & S. Sci.*, May, 1919, p. 191.

social insurance, labor immigration, hours of work and safety. It also demanded the establishment of an international labor office, for the coördination of the labor statistics in various countries, for creation of uniform methods of statistics and for the publication of the collected material. The International Association for Labor Legislation was recommended as the agency for the execution of the above program.[1]

On the last day of October, 1916, copies of this resolution were sent to all national trade unions and labor organizations. The copies were forwarded even to the International Federation of Labor which had its headquarters at Berlin, through the medium of the Scandinavian Federation. The peace demands of February, 1917, issued by this German federation-center were the indirect result of the Leeds resolution.[2]

Early in 1917, the National Executive Committee of the Socialist Party of America sent a cablegram to all the liberal parties in Europe, suggesting an international congress. The proposition was readily agreed to by the Dutch-Scandinavian Committee, and the congress was called to meet in Stockholm in May. The headquarters of the Internationale had been removed to this city early in 1917. Foreseeing the dissension of opinions of delegates from hostile countries, an arrangement had been made beforehand that the delegates from the allied nations and from

[1] See the full text in *U. S. Bureau of Labor Statistics*, bulletin 254, pp. 123-125; The American Federation of Labor was opposed to the Leeds program, see the official correspondence between Ondegeest and Gompers, in *Report of the Executive Council of A. F. of L.*, 1919, p. 53.

[2] *League of Nations*, vol. ii, no. 5, p. 277. During 1916 an international conference met at Lausanne with representatives of 23 nationalities. The object of the conference was to consider the problem of the rights of nations—primarily a political or academic problem rather than any problem affecting labor. See *The World Court*, May, 1918, pp. 305-307.

the central powers should first assemble separately, and should meet conjointly and informally only after reaching some basis of agreement. The delegations from France, Belgium and Germany succeeded in arriving after much delay and difficulty, but the intervention of the allied governments made the conference abortive.[1] However, those who had come, including Scheidemann of Germany, Huysmans, the Secretary of the Internationale, Troelstra of Holland, *etc.*, met informally and conferred under the chairmanship of Branting, the leader of the Swedish party. A promise of success for international conferences was seen in this conference, especially by the onlookers.

About the time of the phenomenal political change in Russia, Arthur Henderson, labor member of the British War Cabinet, visited the prospective Republic of the Soviets. In his tour around the continent he met prominent labor leaders, including Skobelev, Tseretelli, Tchcheidze, and the socialist Minister of Munitions, Albert Thomas of France. Their views on the question of the desirability of an international conference were found then to be in substantial agreement. Consequently on May 9, an official call for such an assembly was issued by the Executive Committee of the Council of the Workers' and Soldiers' Delegates, addressed to all the socialist and labor organizations of the world, to meet in Stockholm between June 28 and July 8, 1917.

The invitation was accepted by the German, Austrian, Hungarian, British, French, Belgian, American and other

[1]The Dutch Federation of Labor sent an invitation with the signature of Ondegeest, secretary of the federation, to Samuel Gompers, president of the A. F. of L., to attend an international congress of national trades federations. On May 4, Gompers sent a letter of refusal stating that American labor had not been previously consulted and that he could "not see how any good could come from our participation in such a conference at this time."

national parties. But the plan did not materialize. The United States took the lead in denying passports to the delegates-elect, who were Morris Hillquit, Victor Berger and Algernon Lee. The Governments of France, Great Britain and Italy followed the example. On October 5, the indefinite postponement of the conference was announced.

During the latter part of September the socialists who had taken part in the Zimmerwald and Kiental Conferences reassembled at Stockholm but the matter discussed then was of no vital significance to international labor.

A gathering which had profound influence upon the international labor situation [1] was called under the auspices of the Swiss Federation of Labor and met at Berne on October 1, 1917. Delegates from the neutral and the central powers, including representatives of the national labor organizations of Germany, Austria, Hungary, Bohemia, Bulgaria, Denmark, Norway, Sweden, the Netherlands and Switzerland participated in the discussion.[2] The conference adopted unanimous resolutions demanding a thorough enforcement of protective labor laws. One of the demands was that "the International Association for Labor Legislation should be explicitly recognized in the peace treaty as the medium for the promotion and enforcement of international protective labor legislation." That "the International Federation of Trades Union be granted representation in the International Labor Office" was another. The resolution also stated the methods of administration, organization and maintenance of the Labor Office.[3]

[1] See *Survey*, March 15, 1917—article on the Berne Conference by L. S. Gannett.

[2] See *Christian Science Monitor*, March 19, 1919, April 12-14, 1919.

[3] *League of Nations*, vol. ii, no. 5, p. 278; for the full text of the resolutions adopted by this Berne Conference, see *U. S. Bureau of Labor Stat. Bull.*, no. 254, pp. 126-129; the American Federation of Labor was opposed to the program of this conference.

In August, 1917, the Inter-Allied Socialist and Labor Conference was held for the second time in London. The American socialists, Hillquit, Berger and Lee would have attended this as well as the Stockholm Conference had they been given their passports. The conference arrived at no common basis of agreement. Then in February, 1918, a third Inter-Allied Socialist and Labor Conference was convoked in the name of the British Labor Party. It met in London, with the majority of the allied nations represented, except Russia, Italy and the United States. The Bolshevik-government refused to participate on the ground that the nature of the conference was at variance with the principles of the Internationale.

The opinion of the conferees as expressed by the labor leaders of the allied nations at this conference has been given wide publicity; its declarations were circulated even on German and Austrian soil.[1] The stand of labor as proclaimed here was substantially the same as that taken at the first London Conference. It was for the league of nations, against secret diplomacy, for the reduction of armaments and against imperialism. The resolution specifically stated the disapproval of economic war after the conclusion of peace. In order to lessen unemployment, the conference advocated regulation of public works throughout the world. An important aspect from our point of view was the claim that labor should be given representation in all deliberative gatherings of the governments. In order to carry this out to practical results, a commission was then appointed consisting of Arthur Henderson of England, Albert Thomas

[1] See "Labor's War Aims: Memorandum on War Aims adopted by the Inter-Allied Labor and Socialist Conference, Feb. 22, 1918." Special bulletin of the International Conciliation, June, 1918; also the *World Court League*, May, 1918, pp. 300-301. See also "La Conference Socialiste Internationale"—article by Jean Longuet in *Le Populaire*, Aug. 15, 1918.

of France, and Emile Vandervelde of Belgium. Their duty was to negotiate with various governments for this purpose.[1] The success which the labor of the world has achieved as the result of persistent agitation may be seen in the Labor Charter in the Covenant of the League of Nations.

4. *The Peace Conference; the Commission on International Labor Legislation; the Labor Charter*

Ever since the signing of the armistice in November, 1918, the Allied Supreme War Council, which had hitherto conducted the military affairs of the allies, was busily engaged in preparations for the Peace Conference. Finally on January 18, 1919, the Peace Conference was opened formally, with the supreme mission to reinstate order and harmony in a war-wrecked world. At the second plenary session of the Conference, which was only a week after the formal opening, a resolution was passed creating a commission to study international labor legislation. It was to consist of two representatives from the five big powers and five from the other powers represented at the Conference. The resolution stated the object of the commission to be as follows:

> . . . to inquire into the conditions of employment from the international aspect, to consider the international means necessary to secure common action on matters affecting conditions of employment and to recommend the form of a permanent agency to continue such inquiry and consideration in coöperation with and under the direction of the League of Nations.[2]

[1] For a summary of the socialist activities so far, see H. Laidler, *op. cit.*, pp. 284-289; also *American Labor Year Book*, 1917-1918, pp. 299-230.

[2] Good documentary sources freely used here for reference on the Commission on International Labor Legislation and its final report are: (1) *American Labor Legislation Review*, August, 1919; (2) *League of Nations*, vol. ii, no. 5, "Labor in the Treaty of Peace," bulletin of the World Peace Foundation.

On January 27, 1919, "the representatives of powers with special interests" held a meeting and agreed that Belgium, on account of her progressive labor legislation, be given two seats on the Commission, and Cuba, Poland and Czecho-Slovakia one seat each. The Commission, as finally appointed on January 31, consisted of the following members:

United States of America:

Samuel Gompers—President of American Federation of Labor.

E. N. Hurley—President of United States Shipping Board.

(Substitutes: H. M. Robinson, Esq., and J. T. Shotwell, Professor, Columbia University.)

Great Britain:

G. N. Barnes—M. P., Member of the War Cabinet.

(Substitutes: H. B. Butler, Assistant Secretary of the Ministry of Labor; Sir Malcolm Delevigue, Assistant Under-Secretary of State, Home Office.)

France:

Colliard—Minister of Labor.

(Substitute: Arthur Fontaine, Counsellor of State, Director of Labor.)

Loucheur—Minister of Industrial Reconstruction.

(Substitute: Léon Jouhaux, General Secretary of the Confédération Générale du Travail.)

Italy:

Baron Mayor des Planches — Ambassador, Commissioner General for Emigration.

Cabrini—Deputy, Vice-President of the Supreme Labor Council.

Japan:

Otchiai—Minister Plenipotentiary of Japan at the Hague.

M. Oka—Formerly Director of Commercial and Industrial Affairs, Department of Agriculture and Commerce.

Belgium:

Vandervelde—Minister of Justice and of State.

(Substitute: La Fontaine, Senator.)

Mahaim—Professor at Liege University.

Cuba:

De Bustamante—Professor at Havana University.

(Substitutes: R. M. Ortiz, Minister Plenipotentiary and De Blanck, Minister Plenipotentiary.)

Poland:

Count Zoltowski—Member of the Polish National Committee; later replaced by S. Patek, Counsellor of the Court of Cassation.

(Substitute: F. Sokal, Director General of Labor.)

Czecho-Slovakia:

Benes—Minister of Foreign Affairs, later replaced by R. Broz.

The President of the Commission was Samuel Gompers of the United States. The Vice-Presidents were G. N. Barnes of Great Britain and Colliard of France. Arthur Fontaine was made the General Secretary and H. B. Butler the assistant to the General Secretary.

The report of the commission was submitted to the Peace Conference, dated March 24, 1919, with the signatures of Samuel Gompers and his staff. The committee recommended in this report the insertion of a section in the Peace Treaty creating an international labor organization and proclaiming nine principles as labor's fundamental rights.

The recommendation was adopted by the Peace Conference. The proposed plan was incorporated in the Peace Treaty [1] as " Part XIII." It is popularly known as the " Labor Charter."

According to this charter, every signatory to the Treaty of Peace and every member of the League of Nations must subscribe to these nine fundamental principles and become a member of the international labor organization. From the point of view of an advocate of labor's " rights " these principles are modest; to forward-looking men whose conception of a complete democracy necessitates full recognition of the proletariat the propositions advanced in this second section of Part Thirteen must seem too moderate and meager. It states only the " minimum " standards to be guaranteed to labor. Nevertheless, for all its limitations, this is the " Magna Carta " of labor. It is an explicit recognition of labor as an indispensable factor in the progress of the world. " Labor's services and sacrifices in the world war," says Dr. John B. Andrews, " and the swelling demands for a new order in which the dearly-won ideals of democracy shall be made everywhere secure, have given an impetus to official action which brings vastly nearer the realization through treaties of an international level of working conditions below which no toiler in any nation shall be allowed to fall and above which continued legislative advances may be more easily and safely achieved by progressive nations." Labor has won its international charter, inscribed in the covenant which federates nations of the earth.[2]

[1] See for the full text of the labor section of the Peace Treaty and the report of this Commission—*League of Nations*, vol. ii, no. 5, "Labor in the Treaty of Peace" published by the World Peace Foundation, 1919, pp. 283-323.

[2] The following words of George N. Barnes, the veteran laborite and

This international labor-guarantee was the result of the century-long struggle of men and organizations which we have traced in the foregoing chapters. But we should not for this reason underrate the achievement of the commission which was charged with the duty of drafting such a charter. The task of the commission was as difficult as it was important. From January 27 till March 24, 1919, they labored, holding in all thirty-five meetings. A number of declarations of principles were proposed at the outset by the delegates of various nations. It was the British and the French proposals which contained plans for a permanent international organization. The plan giving each delegate at international labor assemblies, whether a representative of the government, of capital or of labor, the right to speak and vote individually and not through his national group was in the British proposal. It was adopted on February 12, at the seventh meeting of the commission. The plan should strengthen international bonds since it disregards national obligations. The political genius of the Anglo-Saxon mind secured the great charter of parliamentarism seven centuries ago and now it was again the British that gave to the world this potent means of developing internationalism.

member of the British War Cabinet, who reported to the plenary session of the Peace Conference on behalf of the Commission on International Labor Legislation on April 11, 1919, are of historical significance:

"I need scarcely remind you of the urgency of the work of labor amelioration, for it is well known to all that new thoughts are surging up among us and about us and that the world as a result is in a ferment. Nor need I dwell on its importance, an importance second to only the prevention of war, to which we have already given our hand and seal. Our scheme will, we think, give strength to the League of Nations by enabling it to take root in the daily life of peoples. It will, we believe, give hope and health to those whose lives are scarred by toil and sorrow, and on behalf of the Commission I commend it to your favorable consideration."

For our present purpose, it will suffice to recount briefly the problems which confronted the commission. The British plan was accepted at the outset and made the basis for further procedure, but difficulties were at once encountered in dealing with the counter proposals of the French, Italian, American and other delegations. For instance, the last three delegations, as well as the Cuban, contended that the government-, capital- and labor-delegates at the international labor assemblies should have "equal votes." Their fear was that the workers would never be contented to have the government and capital given three votes which might be combined against their one. It was the practical British mind which foresaw that the government must have two votes against the two votes of capital and labor, since the responsibility for carrying into effect the resolutions of the assembly lay upon the government. The progressive Belgian delegates pointed out also that the votes of the government henceforth would more often be with labor than with capital.

With regard to the matter of procedure: The original British draft provided that any convention adopted by the international labor conference should be ratified by every state which participated in the conference, unless the national legislature rejected it within a year from the time of its adoption by the conference. The French and Italian delegates proposed that a convention should become immediately binding upon the states represented at the conference and that, in case the legislature of the state rejected it, an appeal should be made by the said state to the Executive Council of the League of Nations. Upon examination of the appeal, the Council might submit the case to the Conference for reconsideration. If the original convention were reaffirmed, it should remain effective and no further right of appeal be recognized. The rigidity of the Latin and the elasticity of the British minds had to seek ground for compromise.

A complaint was then made by the American delegation. It brought to the attention of the commission the constitutional obstacle which would prevent delegates from the United States from entering into conventions which infringed in any way upon the rights of constituent states. Article 19 of Part XIII (or 405 of the Peace Treaty) as adopted is the result of the Commission's desperate effort to devise a way out of the dilemma. Under it the decisions of international labor conferences take the form of either recommendations or draft conventions. As regards acceptance or rejection of either of the two forms of decisions States are left practically free, except that an attempt to adopt them must be made by having them submitted to the legislature. In the event of the failure of the legislature to adopt, no further obligation rests upon the state in question. As for the federal states, they are allowed to treat conventions in exactly the same way as recommendations; it should be noted that the federal states are thus under less obligation than other states in so far as their treaty-making powers are more limited. It was added in the report that "the Japanese delegation had abstained from voting on article 19 on the ground that they had not received instructions from their government in the matter." The Italian delegation also did not cast their votes "on the ground of the inadequacy of the powers given to the conference."

The section of the committee's report, dealing with the "enforcement" of the decisions of the conference is interesting from the viewpoint of the technique of international government. We must, however, pass over the details for lack of space, mentioning only the important resolution adopted by the commission. It expressed the hope that the High Contracting Parties might soon come to an agreement which would make conventions of the international labor conferences effective resolutions possessing the force of international law.

While commenting on labor's international charter we should make passing mention of the principles which were proposed for incorporation in the Peace Treaty. The proposals were made by the American, Belgian, British, French and Italian delegations. A series of declarations, originally prepared by the International Association for Labor Legislation, were also submitted by the Swiss Government. The task of the commission was less that of adjusting the varied degrees of standards proposed, since here there was substantial agreement. It was rather that of perfecting the technical elaboration of the varied proposals before they could be submitted for insertion and deciding upon the scope of their application.

The report in its final form was submitted on March 24. It was approved at the fourth plenary session of the Peace Conference on April 11 after a painstaking explanation had been made by George N. Barnes. Before the session closed, a number of comments and suggestions were made in reference to the report, although none spoke disapprovingly. In the absence of Samuel Gompers, President Wilson expressed on behalf of the American workers the sense of gratification over the Great Charter of International Labor.

5. *The Internationals revived (1919) — the Socialist Conference at Berne (Feb. 2-9); the birth of a Student Internationale; the Third Internationale (March 2-6) or the Communist Conference of Moscow*

With the signing of the armistice, war ceased. Statesmen and diplomats were assembled at Paris for the purpose of formulating the terms of peace, but meanwhile the war-worn world was stirring with universal industrial unrest. Stimulated by this circumstance, earnest attempts were made to rehabilitate the old internationals for the liberation of the masses.

On the initiative of the International Socialist Bureau, the first International Socialist Conference since the armistice was held at Berne from February 2 to 9, 1919.[1] Germany, Austria, Holland, Great Britain, France and twenty other countries of the world, representing the total membership of fifty million, sent their delegates. Among the ninety-odd delegates who assembled were Henderson, McDonald, Bunning and Thomas (J. H.) of Great Britain; Haase, Kautsky, Eisner and Janson of Germany; Longuét, Thomas and Renaudel of France; Huysmans of Belgium; Kunfi of Hungary; O'Brien of Ireland; Troelstra of Holland, and men of like renown and mental caliber who had figured in the movement for many years. The countries which refused to participate were Norway, Switzerland, Italy, Serbia, Rumania, Russia and a few others. The Russian Communist Party opposed this conference, fiercely denouncing it as a "yellow internationale." The American delegates were denied their passports and were unable to attend. Australian and Ukranian delegates arrived too late, but Canadian and Argentine delegations were present, representing their comrades across the Atlantic. The agenda of the conference[2] consisted of: (1) responsibility for the war; (2) League of Nations; (3) territorial ques-

[1] For the original speeches and matters relating to the conference, see "The Spirit of the International in Berne"—a pamphlet published by Schloss Steinhof, Lucerne, 1919. A full statement in reference to this conference is contained in the *Report of the Nineteenth Annual Conference of the (British) Labor Party*, Southport, 1919, pp. 218-236.

[2] For a splendid digest of the proceedings of the conference, see Laidler, *op. cit.*, pp. 290-300.

tions; (4) disposition of the prisoners of war; (5) Russian situation; (6) the Labor Charter. Among these the matter of most relevant interest to us is the stand of the conference with regard to the plan of the League of Nations and the Labor Charter. The conference definitely favored a democratic league which shall be representative of, not the governments, but the people. Besides the abolition of standing armies, gradual elimination of armaments, establishment of free trade and international control of oceans and thoroughfares of transportation, it advocated the system of world-distribution of raw materials and food. Arthur Henderson, Mrs. Philip Snowden, and J. H. Thomas of the British Labor Party strongly protested against the old-line spirit of balance of power with armed forces. Complete disarmament was their keynote. Ramsay McDonald clarified British Labor's position toward India and Ireland, demanding for them Home Rule and freedom comparable with all other dominions of the Empire.

The most tangible and direct problem discussed was the Labor Charter. Their demands included a number of practical measures immediately to be instituted, such as compulsory elementary-education and free higher education; eight-hour day; weekly rest period of 36 consecutive hours; prohibition of female night labor; six-hour day for children between 16 and 18 years of age; social insurance system; freedom of association; establishment of employment bureaus; creation of a permanent bureau for internationalization of labor control, *etc.* There were further demands made on the freedom of migration with certain specific provisions. While recognizing the evil of the wage system under which, according to the declaration, labor will be "exploited endlessly by the capitalist class," the conference took the conciliatory view that the evil could be "mitigated by the resistance of organized labor and state intervention."

Shortly after the adjournment of the Berne Conference, a manifesto was issued, dated February 11, 1919, by a group of French students imbued with the spirit of international working-class solidarity. It was addressed to all the socialist undergraduates of the world and declared, among other things:

We pledge ourselves to struggle against the worm eaten structure of capitalism with all the means in our power, through the incessant spread of socialist ideals, through the study of socialism and social problems which continuously confront every thinking man and finally through revolution.[1]

The manifesto aroused great interest in the various countries where it was published, and as a result the *Comité Internationale des Étudiants Socialistes,* with headquarters in Geneva, Switzerland, was created. Arrangements were made to call a congress at Geneva on December 26-29, 1919, in order to create an International Federation of Socialist and Communist Students with various related subjects for consideration.

From March 2 to 6, 1919, a gathering of an extremely radical nature known as the Third Internationale was held in the "powerful Soviet city of Moscow." The conference itself was small numerically, being attended by only 32 delegates, but these represented the discontented left-wing of twelve different countries, including Germany, Hungary, Sweden, Norway, Bulgaria, Rumania, Finland, Ukrania, Armenia, *etc.* Besides the accredited delegates, there were socialist representatives of the United States, Great Britain, France, Switzerland, Holland, Bohemia, Turkey, Jugo-Slavia, Persia, Korea, *etc.*, in attendance without votes. The conference was convoked on the invitation of the Russian communist party, and the prominent figures at the

[1] See *The Socialist Review*, January, 1920, p. 23.

conference were such men as Lenin, Trotzky, Tchicherin and others of the so-called Bolshevik ring. Rakovsky of the Balkan Socialist Federation, Skripnik of Ukrania, Albrecht of the German Spartacan party, Guilban of France and other names which appeared in the list represent the extreme left wing of the socialist movement in their respective countries.[1]

The most important result of the conference was the *Manifesto*[2] which it issued over the signatures of Lenin, Trotzky, Zinovieo, Tchicherin and Fritz Plattan, a Swiss socialist. It is a document recording in forceful terms the bitter revolutionary spirit of the modern communist, with avowed hostility to the existing order, denouncing imperialism as "the root of the world war," and calling again, as did Marx and Engels seventy-two years previously, upon proletarians of all lands to unite. Quite aside from the question of the economic soundness of the assertions contained in this manifesto, the indictment against the world's present-day practices which it presents is significant. It claims, that "the nationalization of economic life, which was so obstinately opposed by capitalist liberalism is now an accepted fact," that "there is no return to free competition, . . . none either to trusts, syndicates or other economic marvels," and finally that:

to bring to an end the prevailing crisis will only be possible with the help of proletarian dictatorship, which will not . . . show consideration for inherited privileges or rights of property but will bear in mind the necessity of saving starving

[1] For detailed record of the conference, see *American Labor Year Book*, 1920, pp. 311-320; also Laidler, pp. 302-307.

[2] Full text of the Manifesto appeared in America in *The Revolutionary Age*—the organ of the Boston local of the Socialist Party, May 10, 1919; also in *The Ohio Socialist*, May 28, 1919; Volkszeitung, May, 1919, *etc.*

multitudes, mobilize all their forces for that purpose, and introduce a general obligation to work and a régime of discipline in work, . . .

6. *The Pan-American labor and socialist movements*

For obvious reasons we have so far avoided the mention of the so-called "international labor unions" in America, but now that the internationalization of the labor movement in America begins to involve not simply the United States and Canada but various other national units, assuming the tremendous form of "pan-American" unionism, we can no longer afford to disregard its significance.

In tracing the development of pan-American labor-unionism one is struck by the singular scarcity of information on the subject, although the movement in this direction must have been under way for some time. As early as November, 1911, there was a Central American Labor Congress held in San Salvador and that might very well be called the precursor of the movement which resulted in the Laredo Conference of November, 1918.[1] This last was the first of the Pan-American Labor Conferences which it was planned to hold annually thereafter. The countries represented besides the United States were Mexico, Columbia, Guatemala, Costa Rica and Salvador. The delegates from Cuba, Peru and Venezuela arrived too late. Argentina, Brazil and Chile failed to send delegates. The American Federation of Labor and the Mexican labor unions were responsible for the convocation of the conference. It lasted three days, from November 13 to 16. The questions of interest which came up for discussion were that of having a Mexican secretary attached to the A. F. of L. head-

[1] For official report with details of the Pan-American Labor Conference, see "Report of the Executive Council of the American Federation of Labor to the 39th Annual Convention, Atlantic City, June 9, 1919," pp. 57-61.

quarters; the locating of representatives of unions of both countries on the border; the removal of the restrictions against Mexican workers joining American unions, *etc.* One dramatic event of the conference was that:

in two great columns, delegates, representatives of the governments of both the Mexican and American republics, and the city officials of Laredo, Texas, and Nuevo-Laredo, Mexico, met at the center of the international bridge which crosses the Rio Grande. There speeches were made by President Gompers, secretary General Morores, General Pablo de la Garza and other officials; the two columns thereupon emerging and returning ranks united, to the Plaza in Laredo, Texas.

As representative of the President of the United States, Secretary of Labor Wilson was present. General Pablo de la Garza, who represented President Carranza of Mexico, also addressed the conference. The whole proceeding aroused tremendous enthusiasm among the labor unions of the surrounding regions. The objects of the Pan-American Federation of Labor were declared to be: [1]

(1) The establishment of better conditions for the working people who emigrate from one country to another.

(2) The establishment of a better understanding and relationship between the peoples of the Pan-American Republics.

(3) To utilize every lawful and honorable means for the protection and promotion of the rights, the interests and the welfare of the peoples of the Pan-American Republics.

(4) To utilize every lawful and honorable means for the purpose of cultivating the most favorable and friendly relationship between the labor movements and the peoples of the Pan-American Republics.

[1] *Op. cit.*, p. 59. Report of the Committee on Permanent Organization. For the full proceedings of the Conference, see ***Pan-American Labor Press***, published by the American Alliance for Labor and Democracy, Dec. 4, 1918, printed in San Antonio, Texas, U. S. A.

Samuel Gompers was elected chairman of the official staff, which consists of a chairman and two secretaries, one English-speaking and the other Spanish-speaking. At the annual congress there are to be at least two delegates from each of the Pan-American Republics.

Further progress of the idea of international action for labor's welfare in America is marked by the historic " Resolution adopted by the American Association for Labor Legislation at the Annual Meeting in Richmond, Va., December 28, 1918." The resolution set forth a program of minimum standards of international labor protection which each country, whether European, Asiatic, American or African should undertake to adopt. On account of its universal importance, the full text of the resolution is reproduced below:

WHEREAS, Maladjustments from which wage-earners suffer, such as inadequate wages, excessive hours of work, unemployment, and industrial accident and disease, are not confined to any one country; and

WHEREAS, These international evils know no frontiers, and national action against them needs to be supplemented and fortified by common agreement on minimum standards of labor conditions below which no person should be required or permitted to work; therefore, be it

Resolved, That the American Association for Labor Legislation urge that in international agreements there be incorporated minimum protective labor guarantees, including:

(1) The principle of the living wage.

(2) Three-shift system in continuous industries and one day's rest in seven in all occupations.

(3) Regulation of working hours for women and young persons, and prohibition of night work by them.

(4) Prohibition of child labor.

(5) Establishment of public employment offices and use of

public work to prevent unemployment during the period of demobilization and other comparatively slack times.

(6) Safety and sanitary devices in industry, and in transportation by land and water, including international use of automatic couplers on railroad trains, and the extension of the Seamen's Act.

(7) Comprehensive systems of social insurance against accident, sickness, unemployment, old age, invalidity, and death.

(8) Provisions for collection and publication of comparable labor statistics through the International Association for Labor Legislation and for the enforcement of international labor regulations through a League of Nations.

It is to be remembered that one outstanding incident of the Laredo Conference was the prolonged debate with reference to the I. W. W. and radicalism. The stand of the American Federation was an exceedingly conservative one. Hardly half a year elapsed after this conference when the first Pan-American Socialist and Labor Congress was called to meet at Buenos Aires from April 26 to May 1, 1919. This conference presented a striking contrast to the Laredo Conference as regards its attitude toward radicalism. Argentina, Bolivia, Chile, Uraguay, Paraguay and Peru were represented. The North American delegates failed to attend. The importance of this congress lay in the unifying of the socialist labor elements of the American continents. The conference cabled greetings to the revolutionary parties of Russia, Germany and Hungary, with words of encouragement for their "efforts to make possible the realization of the ideals of the working class." From the viewpoint of labor legislation, the demands of the conference are still more interesting. They stood for

a 44-hour week, prohibition of child labor, compulsory education to the age of 16, regulation of conditions in shops and factories, minimum wage and the abolition of truck system, bi-weekly payments of wages in currency, elimination of the peonage system, the prohibition of the use of the blacklist, the establishment of labor exchanges and the nationalization of the land.

As the result of the conference an "American Labor and Socialist Secretariat" was established with headquarters at Buenos Aires. The Secretariat under the authorization of the conference acts as the central unifying agency for the labor and socialist activities in the western hemisphere. It publishes a bulletin and is empowered to convoke conferences.

7. *Women's International Congress at Zurich (May 12, 1919); International Federation of Trades Union Congress at Amsterdam (July 25–August 2, 1919)*

On May 12, 1919, the Women's International League met in Congress at Zurich. This, as the official organ of the League declares, "was the first international meeting of organized women which has ever come together to discuss a treaty or to make representations to a Conference of the Powers on the subject of Peace." Women well known in political, literary, educational and social fields assembled as delegates. It was a coincidence that on the very day the Congress met, the terms of the Peace Treaty were published in Paris. Since the Hague Congress of the League in 1915, the women of various countries were making herculean efforts to expedite the coming of peace—and their long-pent-up ideas and idealism found expression at this congress.

Naturally, the main topic of discussion was the peace terms. The Labor Charter, with which we are more closely concerned, was brought up, but soon referred to various national sections for study. Self-determination of peoples, amnesty to political prisoners and conscientious objectors in work-houses, the Feminist Charter, the educational program, *etc.*, were the more important subjects considered. With reference to revolutionary movements, the congress declared "its belief that there is a fundamentally just demand underlying most of the revolutionary movements and its sympathy with the workers who were everywhere seeking to make an end of exploitation and to claim their world." The congress, however, was of course opposed to violence. The delegates "loathing militarism," yet "welcomed the promise of the coming democracy." Jane Addams was the presiding officer. 147 delegates were present, representing 16 European and American countries, including Germany, France, Hungary, Italy, *etc.* The conference lasted five days. President Wilson addressed a letter to the League commenting favorably on its work. It appears to have laid a foundation for important future activities. Since it had little to do directly with labor, we need not go more fully into its proceedings.[1]

An incident of far-reaching importance in the development of the international labor movement which occurred at this period was the reorganization of the International Secretariat. The outbreak of the war had been the direct cause of the disintegration of the old International Federation. The American Federation of Labor, for example, decided against sending fees to the International Secretariat which had its headquarters in Berlin, Germany.[2]

Meanwhile, under the circumstances, Carl Legien, then President of the International Federation of Trades Union,

[1] See *Towards Peace and Freedom*, organ of the League, August, 1919.

[2] The consistent attitude of the A. F. of L. toward the International Federation can be seen in the official correspondence exchanged. It is published in the *American Federationist* for Dec., 1915, Jan., May and November, 1917 and April, 1918; see also Report of the Executive Council, June, 1919.

designated Oudegeest, secretary of the Dutch Federation of Labor to act as temporary secretary of the Secretariat. The agreement reached at this time by the American, British and French national labor federations is noteworthy. They agreed, first of all, that from that time on, whenever war broke out involving the country wherein the headquarters of the International Federation was located, the office should automatically be transferred to a neutral country. Secondly, they concluded that during the existing war the Conféderation Générale du Travail, through its Secretary, Jouhaux, should be the center of correspondence for the labor interests of the Federation.

With the signing of the armistice, overtures were made by the Dutch labor leaders and finally an arrangement was successfully made for holding a congress of the old International Federation of Trades Union at Amsterdam. By this time harmony had been restored in England between the Parliamentary Committee of the British Trade Union Congress and the Executive of the British Federation of Trades Union so that those two bodies shared the representation at the Amsterdam Congress, each taking five of the votes that were allotted to British labor. The American Federation of Labor at its Atlantic City Convention in June, 1919, voted to send a delegation to the congress. Samuel Gompers headed the delegation and was accompanied by Daniel Tobin, John Hynes and Guy Oyster.

The Congress met for the burial of the old International Federation from July 25-26, and then the following Monday, July 28, reconvened for the organization of the new Federation. Eleven national federations were represented by: (1) S. Gompers and D. Tobin, United States; (2) A. Hueber and F. Domes, Austria; (3) C. Martens and G. Solan, Belgium; (4) L. Jouhaux and J. Dumoulin, France; (5) C. Legien and J. Sassenbach, Germany; (6) W. A.

Appleton and B. Tillet, Great Britain; (7) J. Oudegeest and E. Fimmer, Holland; (8) O. Lian and J. Teigin, Norway; (9) F. Caballero and J. Bisteiro, Spain; (10) A. Thorberg and C. Sjostrom, Sweden; (11) K. Dun and C. Schurch, Switzerland.

The Congress opened under the chairmanship of Oudegeest, who continued as the presiding officer throughout the congress.[1] It was on the second day that a heated debate took place on the disloyalty of the German members of the International Federation during the war to the real cause and spirit of the organization. The charge was made by Martens of Belgium. The disruption was brought about apparently because of the dissatisfaction of the congress over the evasive response of Legien, the President of the Secretariat, and Sassenbach, his associate. Jouhaux, Gompers and other members took active part in the acrimonious dispute, till late on Saturday evening, when the old Federation was crushed out of existence.[2]

The new International Federation of Trades Union was brought into being on July 28, 1919, when the congress reconvened at the Concertgebouw, Amsterdam, Holland.[3] It was attended by 14 countries with 92 delegates, representing a total membership of over 17,740,000.

[1] For details of the proceedings of the Congress, see the Report of the A. F. of L. Delegates to the International Federation of Trades Union Congress at Amsterdam, in the *American Federationist*, October, 1919, pp. 921-953.

[2] There was a wide-spread discontent among the members even before the war over the German domination in the international. See articles written by Adolph Smith in the *American Federationist*, Dec., 1919-Feb., 1920; also *Christian Science Monitor*, Oct. 5, 1918, on the "German Control of the International."

[3] The information concerning this congress appeared in New York papers August 1-4, 1919. The cablegrams are dated August 1, United News Service, August 2, Associated Press, *etc.*, all cabled from Amsterdam.

The principal task of the congress was the reorganization of the Federation with a new constitution and by-laws, the election of officers, decision as to the location of the Secretariat, *etc.* The *per capita* tax was fixed at ½ cent per member a year. Thus the American Federation of Labor with its four million members will pay $20,000 per year to the Secretariat. The officers elected were President, W. A. Appleton, England; First Vice-President, L. Jouhaux, France; Second Vice-President, Corneille Martens, Belgium; Treasurer, L. Oudegeest, Holland; Secretary-editor, Edo-Fimmens, Holland. Amsterdam was designated as the location of the headquarters of the Federation.

A committee which had been appointed to consider the Labor Charter, under the chairmanship of the American delegate Hynes declared the insufficiency of the charter in clear terms. The congress thus went on record as being dissatisfied over the Labor section of the Peace Treaty and made sundry demands. Its declarations were on such matters as child and woman labor, the eight-hour day, Sunday rest, home work, right of combination, foreign labor, and minimum wages.

Regarding the Washington Conference of the International Labor Organization under the League of Nations, the congress decided to support it, not because the congress was satisfied with the program but because it considered that "the labor charter may become the basis of a league which will not merely be a league of governments but a league of peoples." [1]

8. *International Socialist Congress at Lucerne (August 2-9); the Student International Congress at Geneva (Dec. 1, 1919)*

While the trade-union leaders of the world were busy

[1] *American Federationist*, Oct., 1919, p. 940.

organizing their Internationale, the "Commission for the Restitution of the Internationale" appointed by the Socialist and Labor Congress at Berne convoked a conference on August 2, 1919, at Lucerne, Switzerland.[1]

The minority group of the Russian socialist parties and Belgian, English, French, Dutch and German delegates came. Arthur Henderson presided over the meeting. Prominent among the delegation were Vandervelde, Bernstein, Troelstra, Tseretelli, Adler, Longuét, McDonald, *etc.* The conference was concerned exclusively with political questions. It issued various demands, such as immediate admission of Germany, Russia, Austria and Hungary into the League of Nations, abolition of military conscription, lifting of the Russian blockade, and withdrawal of financial aid to Denikin and Kolchak.

Upon recommendation of the committee on the Reconstitution of the Internationale it was voted that another congress be convoked on February 2, 1920, at Geneva. To this all the national labor parties of the world were to be invited. An agenda consisting of the internationalist policies on the questions of democracy, peace, dictatorship, nationalization, labor legislation, *etc.*, was adopted for the prospective conference at Geneva.[2]

The Students' Internationale which was launched on the basis of the manifesto of the French socialist undergraduates[3] had further developed before the year closed. Under the auspices of the Bureau at Geneva, a conference was finally called in December. This Geneva conference was

[1] The entire document relating to this conference is compiled in *Report of the 19th Annual Conference of the (British) Labor Party*, Southport, 1919, pp. 218-236.

[2] See *Christian Science Monitor*, Sept. 25, 1919; for comprehensive description see Laidler, *op. cit.*, pp. 300-302.

[3] *Cf.* ch. iv, sec. 5.

the first congress of the Students' Internationale. The discussions which took place related principally to the establishment of a permanent Internationale. Divergence of opinion on the subject of the Third Internationale and communism finally resulted in the creation of two separate bodies. One, known as the "Communist International Students' Federation," is affiliated with the Third Internationale of Moscow. The other association, the "Independent Students' Internationale," aims to unite all socialist and communist students "on the common basis of discussion and mutual relations." [1]

9. *Summary of the historical background of International Labor legislation*

Broadly speaking, there were four distinct currents in the century-long struggle of men to bring about the internationalization of labor standards. Those currents represent the international action of groups or organizations of men of varied philosophies and distinct interests.

The first and preëminently the most striking has been the attitude of the socialist organization, the Internationale. Dating from 1864 when the International Workingmen's Association was first organized by Marx, Engels and other radicals, the rise and fall of the organization has had at least a stimulating effect upon the conservative governments in their formulation of labor policies. The demands which the organization has continually made for the eight-hour day, prohibition of night work of women and children, weekly rest period of 36 consecutive hours, freedom of speech, press and association, and like measures have furnished the legislators with high standards which they

[1] "The Labor News Service," issued by the Press Department, The British Labor Party, 33 Eccleston Square, London, S. W. I.

must endeavor to attain. Before the war the membership of the Internationale was estimated at 12,000,000 or more.[1]

The second current to be noted has been the formation of international trades unions. The movement may be traced back to 1886 when the first trades-union congress of an international character met in Paris. The Zurich Congress of 1897 was a large and important one. The International Federation of Trades Union was organized formally in 1898, and an International Secretariat was then established in Germany as the central executive agency of the Federation. This organization has been primarily interested in trade-union rather than political activities and more conservative than the term unionism is generally construed to imply, although the demands by the workers in mines, railways, and other crafts have often been "the nationalization" of mines, railways and the means of production. Before the war the Federation had nearly thirty national trade-union federations affiliated with it, having a total membership of 7,500,000. Besides the national federations like the A. F. of L., there were thirty-two affiliated craft-union federations. Altogether the organization has held ten international congresses, the most notable ones being the Zurich Congress of 1913, the war-time Berne Congress of October, 1917, the post-war Amsterdam Congress of July, 1919, when reorganization of the Federation took place, and the Washington Conference of October, 1919. The membership in 1919 had reached 17,740,000.[2]

Besides this International Federation there were numerous trade-union federations which were organized on an

[1] This figure is according to Camille Huysmans. See *Socialism in Thought and Action*, p. 290.

[2] See "The Report of the A. F. of L. delegation to the International Federation of Trades Union Congress at Amsterdam" in *American Federationist*, October, 1919, pp. 934-935.

international scale. According to Adolph Smith, who has been officially connected with the Socialist Internationale since its congress of 1882, "there are at least twenty-four trade union internationals. . . . All but four of these Internationals had their headquarters in Germany. Two, the miners' and the cotton operatives', have their headquarters in England with British secretaries. The diamond cutters' International has its offices in Holland and the 'Industry of the Book' (printing trades) in Belgium."[1] If we include the American so-called "international," the aggregate membership of the trade-union internationals must be astonishingly high.

The third of the international currents which has contributed to the internationalization of labor has been the official or governmental movement. The protective labor treaties and agreements which the governments of Europe entered into have of course usually been the result of agitation among unofficial circles and of the conferences of labor-unionists, economists and socialists interested in labor protection. Nevertheless, the merit of the government's good-will must not be underrated. Dating as far back as 1881, when the Swiss government first took steps for an official international labor conference, three official labor conferences met prior to the war, namely the Berlin Congress of 1890 and the Berne Congresses of 1905 and 1913. While due credit must be given to the Emperor of Germany,[2] officials of Belgium, France, *etc.*, the government of Switzerland should, above all, be remembered in the history of international labor legislation as the precursor, promoter and friend of the movement. Before the war, altogether thirty bi-partite agreements in the interests of labor had been signed by twelve European and four non-European states or colonies. The Berne Conference of 1905 resulted in two polypartite treaties of 1906.

[1] See *American Federationist*, February, 1920, p. 176.

[2] See ch. ii, p. 1.

In the preceding chapters we have followed the steps of the governments which resulted in the signing of treaties affecting the interests of workers. The resulting treaties may be classified as:—(1) those providing for the supply or migration of labor; (2) those guaranteeing reciprocal protection to the foreign workers; and, (3) those tending to uniformity of labor standards in the countries concerned.

There were twenty-seven treaties signed before the war, four of which dealt with savings-bank arrangements for emigrants, four others with mutuality of social insurance benefits, and the rest with accident insurance. The treaty creating uniformity of labor standards was the most difficult to bring into being. The only instance of this was the signing of the two conventions at Berne in 1906. The Berne Conventions of 1913 were never formally ratified because of the war.

The fourth and the last current to be mentioned includes the movements which were neither revolutionary nor governmental, and yet were perhaps the most influential of all. Naturally in this class are the groups of individuals and the organizations which are almost totally outside the official or workers' circles and yet tremendously "interested" in reform as a matter of principle or academic concern. The Women's International League for Freedom and Peace, the International Association on Unemployment, the International Committee on Social Insurance, the International Congress on Occupational Disease, and scores of others belong in this class.

The most important of them all is, needless to say, the International Association for Labor Legislation. Since its formation in 1900 in Paris, the association under the leadership of Stephen Bauer has in the course of two decades contributed more than any other association to the cause of higher standards of labor throughout the world.

Regular conferences have been held biennially except during the war. Its publications in French, German and English, containing information on labor legislation, have given great stimulus toward the betterment of labor's status in all countries. It has drafted and prepared international labor conventions and treaties, and the success achieved by the association in bringing into effect the standards which it had advocated has been without parallel. It is especially to be noted that the Berne conventions of 1906 and 1913 were none other than the evidence of the association's fruitful labor. The memorandum submitted by the association to the Swiss government in 1918 was transmitted by the latter to the Peace Conference in order to help in forming the basis of the Labor Charter.

The association at present has twenty-five national sections. Fourteen countries contribute to its maintenance.

In the background of these international labor movements there lurks a revolutionary spirit. The rise of the proletarian dictatorship is seen in the Soviets of Russia, Germany and Hungary, and its widespread influence is being felt in the daily events in all countries. But the problem of international labor remains unsolved.[1]

[1] For a comprehensive summary of the international labor situation, see article by W. Jett Lauck, "International Labor Question" in the *Annals of the American Academy of Political and Social Sciences*, May, 1919, pp. 186-202.

PART II

DIFFICULTIES IN INTERNATIONAL LABOR LEGISLATION

CHAPTER V

Analysis of the Difficulties [1]

1. *Coöperation and Coöperation*

THE difficulties which confront the attempt to legislate for labor on an international scale are manifold, but outstanding obstacles which prevent the nations from uniting on a coöperative basis are the nationalistic spirit of aggression and commercial rivalry.

England's early efforts through factory legislation to protect young apprentices from the exploitation of the ruthless industrialism of the day, were vigorously opposed by the manufacturers whose interests seemed likely to be damaged by the proposed legislation.[2] It is interesting to note that those who protested against the protective labor legislation based their contention upon the plea of national danger. They claimed that such a high standard as was contemplated in the proposed legislation would impose a serious handicap on England in trade competition with the manufactures of other lands with lower labor standards.

" Economic disadvantages—consequent loss in trade and commerce—final downfall of the national industry! " The appeal was thus addressed to the psychology of nationalism.

[1] *Cf.* L. Chatelain, *La Protection internationale ouvrière*, ch. iv, pp. 146-158; P. Boilley, *La Legislation internationale du travail*; G. Adler, *Die Frage des internationalen Arbeiterschutzes*, pp. 54-65; Gustav Cohn, *Die Entwickelung der Bestrebungen für internationalen Arbeiterschutz;* Woolfe, *International Government*, pp. 89-97.

[2] See Hutchins and Harrison, *History of Factory Legislation*, pp. 25-27. We should note in this connection that there was an idea commonly accepted, that it was " cruel to restrict " the laborers' opportunity to work " because they must starve without it."

So long as these antique ideas of national or commercial rivalry prevailed, obstructing the national legislation, it was beyond the sphere of reasonable hopes to bring about international labor legislation.

The prevailing economic dogma of the period, as accepted by most manufacturers and even by average statesmen, was, of course, that the cheaper the expense of production, no matter at what cost to the worker, the higher the ultimate gain to the industry and to the nation.[1]

Factory laws and general legislation in the interests of the workers were accordingly accelerated as soon as it began to be understood that good wages, good hygienic conditions and relatively shorter hours all tend to an increased output and higher industrial efficiency. During the one hundred years since the beginning of labor legislation, enormous masses of evidence have accumulated, supporting the contentions of the reformers who have agitated for the improvement of working conditions.

International labor legislation, as we have already indicated, owes its origin as much to the practical business sense of the philanthropist, Owen, as it does to his high humanitarian motives. Owen, the prophet of Christian socialism, combined to an unusual degree vision with practical judgment.[2] But his proposals did not bear fruit during his life, because the time was not ripe.[3] Nations had to con-

[1] The Act of 1819 was opposed by business men who based their counter-claims on the assumptions: (1) "that the protection and preservation of industry on its commercial side should be the object of the state," and (2) "that the proposed regulation would injure trade and drive it out of the country, eventually reducing not only the capitalists, but also the workers to beggary." See Hutchins, *op. cit.*, p. 27.

[2] See Podmore, *Life of Robert Owen.*

[3] It is a matter of common knowledge that such reforms as were attempted in the Factory Amendment Acts of 1819 and 1825 were both meagre and unsatisfactory. See Hutchins and Harrison, *History of Factory Legislation*, ch. i.

tinue their commercial rivalry and trade competition at the expense of the low-paid, over-worked, undernourished laborers till their suffering and misery took such an aggravated form that the statesmen as well as the manufacturers came gradually to realize the need of some remedy. What was sought by them was therefore a remedy for the existing maladjustment. The relief that they sought was for specific evils [1] in industry rather than the recognition of such modern ideas as the "personality of the worker" and his "inalienable rights." In other words, the basic motive for ameliorating the intolerable conditions of labor lay in the desire to avert the serious consequences of the industrial evil rather than to enhance the standards of the workers as human personalities. In the meantime, the malformation of the industrial growth had already reached what seemed to some an incurable stage. The "Internationale" with its revolutionary doctrine and militant tactics was already formed long before the governments called an international conference to consider the industrial situation. It was more than a generation before the unsuccessful Berlin Congress of 1890 was convoked that a cry was heard: "a Spectre, is haunting Europe—the spectre of Communism!" The governments were slow to awake. They would rather compete than coöperate.

It is now plain that the primary task in the institution of international labor legislation was to bring together the governments at a conference simply to consider the problem. Even this task was by no means easy to perform.[2] The difficulty is amply illustrated by the case of the persistent efforts of the Swiss government which resulted in more failures than successes. After Owen addressed his historic

[1] *Cf. op. cit.*, Introduction by Sidney Webb, p. ix.

[2] See *Archives diplomatiques*, vol. xxxvi, p. 41, *et seq.*, for the attitude of the powers toward the Swiss proposal for conference.

memorial to the congress of potentates at Aix-la-Chapelle, more than two generations passed before the Berlin Congress even with its inadequate preparation was called.[1] More astounding than any other related matter is the fact that it took more than a hundred years after Owen's first call, to assemble the governments of the world even to start a "modest experiment" of world-wide labor regulation. And even this modest attempt came about not as a normal development but as the result of the scourge of God—the World War.

2. *The present world situation and problem*

Thanks to the war, for which we have little else to be grateful, the barriers have at last been removed. The governments of the world have been forced to come together to confer and they have formed a league. In its covenant is the Bill of Rights for the workers of the world. The primary task in instituting an international system of labor legislation has thus been accomplished. At the Congress which will meet annually will sit representatives—not of the governments nor of the workers alone, but of all three of the interests affected — employers, workers and governments. We are now in a position to examine the practical phases of the problem of international labor legislation.

Broadly speaking, the immediate problem of today which challenges any organization for furthering international coöperation is the stupendous one of world reconstruction.[2] But this is beyond the scope of any single agency which man may create. The time element has to enter in. The foundations of civilization which have been so widely

[1] See ch. ii, sec. i.

[2] "The Problems of Reconstruction—International and National" by Lindsay Rogers; published by International Conciliation, February, 1919.

shaken cannot be made firm again in a day. The problem of international labor legislation in order to find practical solution must consequently be approached from the viewpoint of the actual world situation.

One thing is clear: there has been a widespread weakening of labor's stability as the result of the war. Because the lives of millions of workers have been lost and industry has been deprived of its human machinery, immediate action must be taken in every country to increase the output and yet simultaneously to guarantee to the worker high standards of labor conditions. State and society must determine how the living productive forces which are essential to rehabilitation from the destructive results of the war shall be treated. We have to be reminded that the Labor Charter, on which we have frequently commented with enthusiasm, lays down after all only a " meagre minimum " as Sidney Webb calls it, and that the expressions of the organized workers of the world on this bill have been far from those of unbounded joy.[1] As a matter of fact many progressive labor organizations, like the American Federation of Labor, have placed on record their dissatisfaction, while the radical or " red " organizations have scorned it from the outset.[2]

These differences, which prevent the establishment of a cordial *esprit de corps* and unanimity of action in reference to international labor legislation, oppose serious practical difficulties to its progress. Other practical difficulties are

[1] See *American Federationist*, Oct., 1919, pp. 938-939. The International Federation of Trades Union Congress with its 18,000,000 membership passed a resolution disapproving the charter by a vote of 31 to 20. Also *International Review*, June, 1919, pp. 501-504.

[2] See the accounts of the conferences at Stockholm, Zimmerwald, Kiental, Berne, Lucerne, Moscow, *etc.*, in ch. iv. Also for a valuable documentary source, see "Labour and the Peace Treaty—an Examination of Labour's Declaration and the Treaty Terms" published by the British Labor Party, 1920.

found in the differences in the conditions that obtain in various countries, politically, economically and climatically. Of these, the economic conditions seem to be the predominant factor obstructing the development of international coöperation, although day by day and month by month the world is becoming economically more interdependent.[1]

3. *Geographic differences* [2]

It goes without saying that there are peoples whose economic life depends largely on their natural location or geographic environment. The climate, the soil, the contour of the land and the like play an important rôle in conditioning the mode of industrial life. An attempt to set up literal uniformity of standards in the labor laws of all lands is destined to result in failure.[3] This obvious fact was recognized early. At the Paris Peace Conference the British proposal of the labor section of the treaty contained a clause purporting to avert the difficulty.[4]

We have already commented on the great ingenuity of the British draft. It was devised adroitly to avert the difficulty, in which the colonies scattered over the earth would be involved if a high labor standard were universally imposed. But we must note one important feature of this draft. If the goal of international legislation is a "uniform standard" in any sense of the term, there is in it a clause which con-

[1] See "International Economics," *Annals of the American Academy of Political and Social Sciences*, May, 1919.

[2] See Chatelain, *op. cit.*, pp. 147-149.

[3] See Dwight T. Farnum's article in *The Nation's Business*, published by U. S. Chamber of Commerce, March, 1920, pp. 24-25. Mr. Farnum says: "Climate is a great enemy to standardization. Several hours relaxation in the middle of the day is necessary under the tropics. A siesta in Norway would result in the loss of most of the daylight hours during half a year. The amount of work done per hour is directly affected by the climate. This governs the output. . ."

[4] See *Peace Treaty*, pt. xiii, article 405.

tradicts itself.[1] It may in time be resorted to to defeat to some extent the purpose of international labor legislation. However, this amounts only to a rather fine point of legalism. From the broader outlook of the effort to bring about some sort of international agreement, it was absolutely necessary to insert a provision of this description, so as to avoid fatal rigidity. If the principle of compromise affords solution of any problem, the difficulty which is due to climatic or geographic differences is met by giving "due regard . . . . to the climatic conditions which make the industrial life of the people [of different countries] substantially different."

4. *Legal or constitutional differences*

Another difficulty results from differences in the constitutions and legal systems of different countries.[2] Without attempting to go into technicalities, we may simply observe that in the case of the federal states, for example, it often happens that the federal authorities may agree to certain terms of a treaty without any assurance whatever that these will be either accepted or enforced by the different states of the union. An example is furnished by the case of the United States of America. The question as to the power of the United States under her constitution to enter into labor treaties was a baffling one to the Commission on International Labor Legislation at the peace conference.[3] Can a treaty embodying the action of an international legislature be constitutionally ratified by the federal government of the United States and if so, can Congress pass the laws necessary to carry it out? This was a question of no small

[1] See ch. viii, sec. 2-6.

[2] *Cf. Chatelain*, pp. 149-151.

[3] See the *Report of the Commission*, ch. ii, 1 Procedure (Articles 14 to 21).

consequence, because upon it depended in large measure the effectiveness and binding force of international labor legislation.[1]

Under the constitution of the United States[2] the President is authorized to make treaties with the approval by two-thirds vote of the senate. Elsewhere in the constitution,[3] the states are forbidden to enter into treaties, or even into any agreement or compact with a foreign power without the consent of the Congress. Thus it is clear that the United States has to be a single unit in the matter of treaty making with an outside power. Moreover, according to another clause of the constitution, "all treaties made . . . . under the authority of the United states" become the "supreme law of the land."[4] The crux of the situation lies not in the absence of power in the federal government to make treaties but in the fact that it is a government whose jurisdiction is limited to the subjects entrusted to it, expressly or by implication, by the Constitution, jurisdiction over other subjects being reserved to the states. To determine whether in the making of any law or treaty the federal government has exceeded its constitutional ability is the duty of the Supreme Court which is required by art. III, sec. 2 to extend "to all cases in law and equity, arising under the Constitution, the laws of the United States and *treaties made, or which shall be made*, under their authority." Clearly then decision of the issue will depend upon the attitude of the judiciary rather than upon the claims of those who uphold the "states rights" and oppose all federal

[1] See the enlightening discussion on this question by F. P. Chamberlain, *Proceedings of the Academy of Political Science*, vol. viii, no. 3, pp. 90-100, or, *Labor Legislation Review*, vol. ix, no. 3, pp. 330-338.

[2] Article ii, sec. 2.

[3] Article i, sec. 10.

[4] Aticle vi, clause 2.

actions tending to infringe upon the states "autonomy" in legislation. The precedents thus far established in the United States indicate[1] the encouraging fact that in practically all cases the treaties in preference to the powers reserved to the states, have been upheld by the Court whenever conflicts have arisen between the treaty provisions and the state statutes.

In order to allow more freedom of action to federal governments similarly situated as the United States, a new development, by way of adjustment, will perhaps be necessary either nationally or internationally. But it is clear that even the constitutional difficulty which avowedly is a strong argument against the internationalization of standards, may be overcome.

5. *Social tradition; prejudice and ignorance*

In spite of the war among nations and friction among races of men, there is no denying the fact that cosmopolitanism is increasing. Internationalism is the general trend of the world and so the difficulties which are due to geographic, or even constitutional, differences are likely to diminish. A difficulty which is more subtle and deep-seated lies in the unseen lines of social cleavage and the intangible realm of prejudice and ignorance.[2]

The forces of opposition at work are innumerable but it seems that more harm results rather from the prejudiced "savants," who see only faults magnified rather than from the profoundly ignorant masses. Rolin Jucquemyns, writing

[1] See Chamberlain, *op. cit.*, pp. 332-335.

[2] There are of course other difficulties which are exceedingly important, besides those enumerated. They are dealt with in the following chapters separately. See in this connection, Chatelain's critical examination of Leroy-Beaulieu's objections against international regulation of labor, in *La Protection internationale ouvrière*, pp. 153-158.

about the Berlin Congress of 1890 in *Revue de droit international et de legislation comparée* referred to it as " Socialism in the international labor conference." For him things "proved" that it was " nothing but a gathering of socialists." Certain United States Senators regarded the Washington Conference with no less fear and suspicion than did this French writer the Berlin Conference.[1]

To many conservative minds the shock of having labor matters discussed together with the dignified affairs of diplomacy was overwhelming. Alphonse Rivier's expression of his unpleasant surprise illustrates the point. He feared "*. . . . de voir ainsi transporter dans le domaine de droit des gens certaines eutopies qui jusqu'a present ne peuvent exercer leurs ravages que dans quelques legislations nationales.*" [2] It may be that this was a sense of refinement rather than primitive fear, for we notice even in Prof. Mahaim's masterly treatise, *Le Droit international ouvrier,* apologetic introductory excuses for the title of the book which combines the dignified phrase "*Le Droit international*" with the plebeian "*ouvrier.*" He takes the trouble of explaining that this combination is not his own but that it was made by some one else at an earlier date [3] and that the combination sounds at first queer and inappropriate but that *cette alliance de mots est un signe des temps!* [4]

Even more amusing to our mind today is the typical de-

[1] See ch. vii; also see Dr. J. B. Andrews' reference to Senator C. Lodge's attitude in *Proceedings of American Academy of Political and Social Sciences,* July, 1919.

[2] *Principes de droit de gens,* vol. i, p. 362.

[3] B. Raynaud's *Le Droit international ouvrier* was published in Paris, 1906.

[4] Mahaim, *op. cit., Introduction,* pp. 1-3.

clamation of a celebrated writer [1] in reference to the Berlin Congress of 1890:

> Can we imagine General Caprivi or the Marquis of Rudini addressing diplomatic notes to the Quai d'Orsay on the carrying out of international arrangements concerning the length of the working day? Let us not harbor ideas which are illusions or at least premature; such agreements would be more difficult to formulate and scarcely less dangerous in their application than a general disarmament treaty signed in Paris or Berlin. But in order to climb the long steep path of social progress is it really necessary that different states be bound by treaties? Thank God, it is not!

Now the nature of this difficulty is clear. As institutions with a long history are often revered simply on the ground that they are old, so those that are new are just as often slightingly received either with suspicion or at best, with sceptical curiosity, if they are not flatly rejected, because they are "new and untried." This difficulty, unlike wartime reaction, will remain ever present, retarding the rapid progress of reform. But a difficulty of this nature oftentimes acts as an anchor of safety, giving security to the institutions that have been established for the well-being of man.

6. *Difficulty imbedded in the economic system*

Finally, in recounting the difficulties which obstruct the course of international labor legislation, we must give due consideration to the difficulties which have their roots in the industrial system itself.[2]

[1] Leroy Beaulieu in *La Papauté, le socialisme et la democratie*, 3rd ed., Paris, 1892, pp. 175-176, cited by Stephen Bauer, Bull. 254, p. 8 of *U. S. Bur. of Lab. Stat.*

[2] For an enlightening discourse on this entire subject, see *The New Social Order*, by Harry F. Ward.

The problem of international labor legislation is naturally more complex than the problem of labor protection within a nation. A failure to view the problem broadly is bound to result in grave errors in its practical solution. If labor legislation within the state is to maintain industrial efficiency and to protect the rights and interests of the workers, international labor legislation must provide an economic foundation for international peace.[1]

Based upon such a broad hypothesis, the analysis of the problem must take into consideration not simply its practical aspects, such as the differences of climate, political institutions and industrial development, but also the theoretical aspects of the labor problem which have of late become even more acute. This difficulty is voiced by the critics of the modern economic system. Their views must not be disregarded as merely destructive because they are forsooth revolutionary in their conclusions.[2]

We should consider in the first place the possible limitations of international labor legislation which is based on the scheme which the League of Nations' Covenant provides.[3] The organ of international labor legislation which the scheme contemplates is to serve as a means for adjusting the unevenness of progress of labor legislation in the different nations, for bringing about uniformity of labor standards in all lands and for agreeing upon reciprocity of protection of foreign workers by guaranteeing equal protective treatment to both native and alien labor. Accordingly, it will

[1] See Garvin, *Economic Foundation of Peace*, Macmillan, 1919.

[2] See Henderson, *Aims of Labor*, Huebsch, New York, 1918, especially, appendix II, "Labor and New Social Order," pp. 98-106; also the Russian Documents by International Conciliation, March, 1919.

[3] A suggestive essay on this matter is "Socialism and the League of Nations" by E. C. Fairchild, published by the British Socialist Party, *International Socialist Library*, no. 10.

undertake to fix the maximum hours beyond which men shall not be emplowed. It will fix the method whereby violations of the agreement are properly reproved or penalized. It may dictate the minimum age below which a child shall not be admitted to industrial employment. It may even recommend a certain amount of money payment as the minimum of wages to be paid to the worker. Even when legislation goes so far as to institute a thorough international system of insurance against illness, accident, death and unemployment, difficulties will probably still exist.

It will plainly be a blunder if the international statesman of today undertakes merely to suppress a liberal movement, because he regards the movement as *per se* a danger to the peace and order of the world, and fails to remove the conditions which necessitated or at least justified its germination and growth.[1]

In his monumental work *The Economic Foundation of Peace,* J. L. Garvin has pointed out the significant fact that the signature of one of the belligerents, Russia, does not appear on the Peace Treaty at all. The treaty and the situation it creates cannot be adequately dealt with in the absence of that nation. Garvin's assertion in this connection is worthy of our attention. He says: "The real key to the future does not lie in Germany. It lies in Russia. That is the acid test of the Allies' capacity. There can be no basis of natural stability in the world until a strong and free Russia is restored and brought fully into the League of Nations." Our reasoning henceforth must proceed to the "whys" and "wherefores" for labor's emphatic stand on the Russian policy and we must soon recognize it as "the key to the future of industrial democracy throughout the world."

[1] See "Labor and the Peace Treaty" published by the British Labor Party, pt. iii, pp. 55-64.

It is not within the province of our present inquiry to criticize either the present system of production or the proposed schemes of coöperative commonwealths. However, in order to cope with the problem involved in the universal cleavage between capital and labor, nothing short of a thorough plan of industrial democracy can be adequate, and therein will be found the ultimate function of international labor legislation.[1]

[1] See *Democracy in Reconstruction*, by Cleveland and Shafer, Houghton, Mifflin Co., 1919, pts. iii-v, inclusive.

CHAPTER VI

Varied Economic Conditions

1. *The economic barriers*

"The removal.... of all economic barriers and the establishment of an equality of trade conditions among all nations"[1]—this is a fair but alas an empty phrase, so long as the plan of international economic coöperation, is not "given a structure of force and reality."

We must not forget that it was primarily the fatality of the war which quickened into life the movement toward international coöperation.[2] It was not idealism but the fear of a common danger which brought the allied powers to the basis of a close economic coöperation. The coöperation which resulted was neither universal nor long-enduring. Like many other good and commendable schemes to which the desperate situation of war-time gave birth, the removal of economic barriers which was achieved for the duration of the war seems to have been destined to terminate with the war. There are indications that the war ended not with "a peace without victory" but with "a victory without peace."[3] During the war in the matter of the securing, allocation and transport of supplies of food stuffs and raw materials, the allied nations and "sympathetic" neutrals showed a wonderful spirit of coöperation, and the manner in

[1] No. 3 of President Wilson's Fourteen Points.

[2] For a clear presentation of the Allies' success in coöperation, see J. L. Garvin, "Economic Foundation of Peace," ch. iv, pp. 55-74.

[3] See *The Nation*, "International Relations Section," April 19, 1919; also Garvin, *op. cit.*, pp. 75-87.

which the International Munitions Council and the Supreme Economic Council operated within their respective spheres was a marvel. But, as soon as the armistice was signed the old spirit of conflict instead of conciliation returned. For more than a year the starving millions in certain European countries were left without food and the people outside with surplus of raw material and foodstuffs were forbidden to feed them or to trade with them.

These were of course "abnormal" conditions growing out of the exigencies of the war. What has been the general condition of economic relationship among the industrial nations in the so-called "normal" peace times? Admittedly there are two sides to the question but no one will deny the prominence of "tariff wars, struggle for concessions, spheres of influence and peaceful penetration,—to which should be added the rivalries in international financing."[1] One outstanding feature at least, in peace times, of the international economic situation has been that of intense competition for colonies and for markets. The observation would almost seem to be justified that no sooner does the industrial development of any nation reach a certain stage, than a relentless outside pressure begins in order to keep the industrial machinery going. The increase and surplus of capital likewise seem to result in pressure tending to intensify international economic competition.

What is to be the remedy? It is obviously the function of international labor legislation to find a common ground of economic activity to alleviate the ill-effects. First of all, a means must be found for regulating the labor standards. The greatest task of international labor legislation consists in setting up standards which are agreeable to all, and thus

[1] See "Economic Internationalism" by E. M. Patterson, pp. 4-5 in the *Annals of the American Academy of Political and Social Sciences*, May, 1919; also Garvin, *op. cit.*, pp. 1-55.

the practical difficulty is of adjusting varied industrial conditions, unevenness of progress, divergent degrees of experience in labor legislation, the absence or inadequate foundation of labor organizations and other economic diversities.

2. Hours of work; present legal status; extent of 8-hour day in practice

It is beyond the scope of this monograph to give an exhaustive comparative study of the conditions as regards hours of labor that obtain in different countries. It suffices merely to illustrate the difficulty of setting up a reasonable minimum standard to consider briefly the problems which the Washington conference of 1919 undertook to solve. For this purpose we find in "Reports I to IV" of the "Organizing Committee[1] for the International Labor Conference at Washington, 1919," a mass of comprehensive and illuminating material.

The universal eight-hour day has long been a demand of the workers of the world. We have already observed among the "General Principles" laid down in the Labor Charter of the Covenant of the League of Nations this principle enunciated as one "of special and urgent importance."[2] Naturally the 8-hour day or 48-hour week was to be the standard insisted upon by the international organ of labor legislation, but even the "process of realization" of this minimum has seemed for years to be slow and reluctant.[3] Up to the outbreak of the war, this was only a "ten-

[1] See ch. vii, sec. 1, for composition, work, *etc.*, of the committee. Henceforth in our notation *Report* refers to the Report of this committee.

[2] Article 427 of the Peace Treaty.

[3] In this connection, see a valuable contribution by Leifur Magnusson of the U. S. Bureau of Labor Statistics, entitled "Hours of Labor in Foreign Countries" in *Annals of Am. Acad. of Pol. and Soc. Sci.*, May, 1919, pp. 202-232.

dency." But the Allied and Associated Powers had explicitly recognized that they "should endeavor to apply [this principle] so far as their special circumstances will permit," and since the signing of the armistice there has been encouragingly wide expansion of 8-hour laws. Attention should be called to the fact that what is laid down in the Peace Treaty (article 427) with regard to the 8-hour day or 48-hour week is not to be merely a "standard" or "basic" limit upon which normal wages are calculated and which demarcates the point at which the overtime pay at increased rates is to begin. The purpose of this provision was to preclude all possibilities of longer hours which will result in undue fatigue and other attendant evils, subject only to the restraint caused by the wage bargain between the employer and worker. It aims, in other words, to insure to the worker definite leisure and opportunities for recreation and social life.[1] Present laws and practices in various countries are by no means in harmony with such a principle.[2] The laws limiting the working hours are of three types.[3]

The first type is illustrated by the Czecho-Slovakian Eight Hours Act of 1918 which limits working hours to 8 a day or 48 a week or to their equivalent, averaged over a longer period and specifies the industries to which the law should apply. To this class belong the laws of six countries: Czecho-Slovakia, the Netherlands, Norway, Switzerland, Uruguay and New Zealand.

The second type is that most commonly in operation, and is the recognition by law of the 8-hour day or 48-hour week as the general rule. It is far less rigid than the first type, leaving the application of the general principle

[1] *Report i*, pp. 2-3.

[2] For a brief and yet suggestive summary, see *American Labor Legislation Review*, September, 1919, pp. 304-307.

[3] *Report i*, p. 5, *et seq.*

with any necessary modifications to special decrees or acts. Of this type are the laws in force in ten countries: Germany, German-Austria, France, Russia, Finland, Spain, Portugal, Poland, Panama and Ecuador.

The third type includes the most liberal laws of industrial adjustment in existence, which recognize as legally binding the decisions arrived at through arbitration or permit collective bargaining. There all industrial issues including questions in regard to the limitation of working hours are settled by arbitration or by collective agreement. The constituent states of the Australian commonwealth,[1] certain states of the American union [2] and certain Canadian provinces have already enacted laws or developed practices of this last progressive type.

Eight-hour laws, as commonly understood, have operated in New South Wales and New Zealand for a number of years but in most outside states the experience has been brief, being confined in many cases to the period since the war, *e. g.*, Germany, France, Russia, Norway, the Netherlands, Switzerland, Spain, Portugal, Panama, Ecuador and Uruguay. In Great Britain, Belgium and Denmark bills of this category have been presented and await action by the legislature. In the United States the famous "ten-hour laws" of Oregon and the similar law of Mississippi have been sustained by the Supreme Court, but generally speaking the general eight-hour law is still a precious boon vigorously fought for by the unions in the United States.[3]

[1] Queensland, New South Wales, Victoria, South and West Australia, Tasmania.

[2] New York, Massachusetts, New Jersey, Ohio, Wisconsin, Illinois, Indiana, Missouri, *etc.*, see Groat, *Organized Labor in America*, pp. 217-235.

[3] The American Federation of Labor has fought for it for over 40 years. See speech by S. Gompers, *Proceedings of the Washington Conference*, Provisional Record, Nov. 5, 1919, pp. 60-61.

In all cases the law provides for overtime. It is perhaps no exaggeration to say that most of the legislation on the 8-hour day or 48-hour week consists of exceptions rather than of the statement of the principle itself.[1] As in the case of the French Eight Hours Act, the details of exceptions are to be in most instances provided by Administrative Orders. The exceptions may be classified as either permanent or temporary but such a distinction is not always clearly set forth in the laws.

Overtime is almost universally allowed as a matter of explicit exception in the law in cases of national emergency. In case of accidents as in other unforeseen circumstances also the law may be suspended. In the United Kingdom, in many states of the American union and practically everywhere these cases may be cited. *Force Majeure* is an imperative term appearing in the labor laws of European states with the power of suspending all legal limitation of working hours. It is a general practice also to permit by law overtime work involved in the preparation or completion of certain processes necessary to be done either before or after the main work. Even in the radically progressive law of Czecho-Slovakia, "no special permission (is needed) for such subsidary operations which necessarily precede or follow the work such as the heating of boilers, cleaning the workrooms, feeding animals, *etc.*, even when they are carried on outside the ordinary hours of work fixed in the undertaking." [2]

Longer hours are permitted also to the watchmen, signalmen on railroads, *etc.*, whose work is obviously "light" or "intermittent." In the Netherlands for example "men who are engaged solely in caretakers' duty" are allowed to

[1] *Report i*, pp. 15-108.

[2] *Ibid.*, p. 31. Factory Law of Czecko-Slovakia, article 7, (i).

work as long as 13 hours per day or 78 hours per week. "Adjustment of shifts" is another item calling for an exception from the general working-hour law. It is obvious that in order to carry on a process which requires continuous operation without interruption the shifts must be overlapped. Work somewhat in excess of the normal period will *have to be* allowed to permit the changing of shifts. "Seasonal trades" offer still another important item of exception. The overtime allowed is generally subject to a maximum limit such as 21 days (German-Austria), 24 days (The Netherlands), 28 days (Denmark), *etc.* The law is not stringent where the work of the season does not prolong the overtime to any serious extent. Mere notification to the authorities suffices in German-Austria even when the overwork lasts as long as three days in a month.

Generally speaking, then, it appears that the problem of overtime is met by granting a specified number of days on a limited duration of time during the year. It should be understood, however, that the legal requirement of increased rates of pay for overtime work is also a device to control overtime in the interests of the worker. This device is resorted to most extensively in the Australian commonwealths where organized labor is active and the awards of wage boards are legally binding. In the United States the Oregon law (sec. 4) requires "double time" for overtime. The law of Queensland is interesting. There the legal hours[1] may be exceeded to 57 "in order to meet an unforeseen pressure of work" provided that (1) 48 hours be not exceeded more than 8 times a year; (2) "time and half and *one shilling* of "tea money" be paid; (3) the worker consents to overtime employment, and finally (4) that the labor department be notified with the payment of a

[1] *Repcrt i*, p. 48.

fee of two shillings and six pence. The law of Ecuador is still more interesting. It specifies the hours to which overtime may extend, with the payment of wages at the increased rates of 20 to 100 per cent in proportion to the amount of the overtime work.

In addition to these, many states require the authorization by competent authority for overtime and also their laws lay down the limits to overtime. The examples are: " 240 hours during 20 weeks " in Czecho-Slovakia, " 2 hours a day for 24 days in a year " in Switzerland; " 2 hours a day on 60 days in a year " in the tobacco stores in Greece; " 1 hour a day in 60 days in a year " in the coal mines in Great Britain, *etc.*

There are also laws requiring the record of all overtime work, to be entered and kept for inspection by the authorities.[1] They furnish plainly another channel for the control of overtime.

Laws limiting the working hours to eight in certain specified industries only are found practically everywhere. The eight-hour laws applying only to the mines and dangerous trades are common even among the "less advanced" states outside of Europe. Miners, public employees, and other employees engaged on public works in the United States are generally subject to the eight-hour standard; under the Adamson law employees engaged in operating railroads have also been brought under the same standard.

Where legal restraint is absent, the limitation has been brought about extensively by the method of collective agreement as indicated summarily at the beginning of our study on this matter. This has been particularly true in the United States, in Australia and elsewhere where labor's combination was legally feasible and effective in practice.[2]

[1] *Report i*, pp. 50-52.

[2] *Ibid.*, pp. 55-65.

But this statement would apply only to Europe, certain sections of America and Australia. There is a vast population protected by neither statutory provisions nor social regulation of industrial conditions.[1] The workers of Japan, China, India, Siam, Persia, and elsewhere, numbering millions, are largely unprotected. The problem is stupendous.

3. *Unemployment; the extent of the problem; and its solution*

The problem of unemployment is both chronic and wide spread. The surpassing importance of this "most subtle and pervading disease of the present industrial system" can scarcely be overrated. As the result of an extensive and painstaking inquiry made by the Organizing Committee for the Washington Conference, it was concluded that, within each nation, "the normal results of unemployment are poverty, overcrowding, disease, incompetence and lack of energy, expense to the State and unrest." Further it was established that internationally, "the results of unemployment in each country diminish the market for foreign goods in that country and weaken the power of exporting from every country in which unemployment is serious."[2] Thus unemployment leads to tariffs and protection in order to combat and prevent imports, which in turn will create unemployment abroad. Unrest, lawlessness, crime and revolution all seem to be in close propinquity to the phenomenon of unemployment. The nature of the problem lends itself most strongly to the plea for revolutionary schemes of social reform.[3]

[1] *Report iv*, pp. 5-10.

[2] *Report ii*, p. 23.

[3] Adverse criticism against the present industrial system on account of widespread unemployment should not be regarded as the point of view of only the irresponsible revolutionist. The French government

The scope of the problem, as revealed by recent statistical information, is an unsatisfactory basis for study because the war has caused abnormal fluctuations in the status of work in general. Moreover we may feel assured that no institution, including industry and methods of production, will be restored completely to pre-war conditions. Nevertheless the causes of unemployment, deep-seated and inherent in the system, have remained unchanged. We must reasonably expect the recurrence of "the cyclical depressions of industry," "seasonal fluctuations," "the chronic under-employment of casual labor" and "displacement of workers by changes in industrial processes." The present problem is not that of providing mere relief to the unemployed but of establishing a comprehensive method of prevention on an international scale.

The problem has been intensively studied both nationally and internationally. In practically every industrialized country, statistical study and publication of the information by the state bureau or similar authority have been made.[1] *L'Association internationale pour la lutte contre le Chômage* was organized September 21,1910, with its headquarters at Ghent. Prior to its formal organization, the first international conference was held at Milan in 1906, succeeded by another in Paris in 1910 and up to the outbreak of the war, an international conference on unemployment had been held annually. Sixteen countries had national sections[2] and

among others pointed out that "the character of the problem of unemployment is such that it cannot be viewed in isolation from the wage system as a whole and the social and industrial organization at the moment prevalent in most countries." *Report ii*, p. 7.

[1] *Report ii*, pp. 28-29, contains the list of publications in 15 countries giving statistical information on the subject.

[2] U. S., Austria, Belgium, Great Britain, Denmark, France, Holland, Italy, Finland, Germany, Hungary, Luxemburg, Norway, Sweden, Switzerland and Spain.

six countries maintained correspondents[1] of this organization.

The figures obtained before the war for a number of years in different countries present a picture which is rather a sad commentary on the industrial life of many nations. The United States of America, for example, known generally as the "land of opportunities," shows acute fluctuation in employment figures, with the percentage of the unemployed workers normally three times as great as in either England or Germany.[2] Even in the iron and steel industry which must maintain a comparatively more stable force of workers, the difference of figures of the employed during the busiest and slackest seasons shows as high a percentage as 40. The mean precentage of workers of several unions who were unemployed during the ten years (1904-13) before the war, was found to be as follows: U. S. A. (New York State) 15.2; Belgium 2.7; United Kingdom 4.7; Austria 5.7; France 7.8; Denmark 9.5; Norway 3.1; Germany 2.1. The fact that certain trades are essentially seasonal and are subject to the iron law of joblessness during certain seasons in every country is illustrated in the table below, which applies to certain occupations in the building trades.

It is not within the purview of our study to present in detail either the extent or various phases of unemployment. It is essential, however, that we comprehend them as the basis of further consideration—especially to inquire into the causes of unemployment.[3] Sickness, old age, imbecility

[1] Australia, Canada, New Zealand, Roumania, Argentine and Japan.

[2] *Report ii*, p. 13, also p. 16; also, *Unemployment in United States*, 1916; *Labor Bulletin of the United States Bureau of Labor Statistics*, no. 195, p. 23; *Employment Service Bulletin* (weekly) published by the U. S. Department of Labor.

[3] For an enlightening discussion of this problem, see *Proceedings of the National Conference of Charities and Correction*, Baltimore, 1915,

PERCENTAGES UNEMPLOYED IN BUILDING TRADES

Months.	United Kingdom, 1913-14.	Germany, 1912-14.	Holland, 1911-12.	Belgium, 1911.
January	8.7	12.3	14.9	23.1
February	6.8	13.8	12.1	21.9
March	4.9	11.4	4.1	4.1
April	3.8	11.3	2.0	1.1
May	3.5	7.8	1.5	0.9
June	3.7	6.9	1.6	1.3
July	3.9	5.2	2.2	0.9
August	4.9	5.1	2.2	0.4
September	5.2	5.7	2.6	0.7
October	5.1	6.7	3.0	0.8
November	5.7	7.7	5.9	2.9
December	6.0	11.6	8.8	7.0
Average	5.2	8.8	5.1	5.4

and defective physical conditions as well as the aversion to work—all contribute to the unemployable class but the consideration of them may very profitably be excluded. The most obvious cause of unemployment is fluctuations of trade due to changes of weather and seasons, unregulated production, social habits, *etc.* Specialization of trade is another cause, in that it tends to render labor "immobile." The production only "to order" or to meet a sudden "fashion" is also a serious cause of rush and depression of employment.

Some of these conditions may be partially eradicated by instituting a state system of control, but certain others are apparently beyond control. No single measure to combat the problem will suffice. The regulation of employment through the medium of a thorough state system of em-

address by Prof. H. R. Seager, entitled "Unemployment: Problem and Remedies." Reprinted as no. 42 of the reprint series, published by the office of the Conference, 315 Plymouth Court, Chicago, Ill.

ployment exchanges is a method adopted by the various industrial nations in their legislation.[1] This method of prevention coupled with a system of unemployment insurance as a relief measure may be suggested as a partial solution of the problem within the nation. But the real service of international labor legislation extends beyond either measure.

It need not be pointed out here that the function of international labor legislation is not merely to set up or recommend legislative measures to be adopted separately in each country. In this age of world interdependence, of exchange and communication, the economic forces which cross frontiers must increasingly be controlled by international action. In order to attack the root of the problem of unemployment, and to avoid international financial crises, opportunites for employment should if possible be provided through international coöperation. It is not only desirable but inevitable that international labor legislation should undertake to regulate the flow of both human labor and material resources across national boundaries. Thus it would appear that there are ultimately two alternatives in the solution of the unemployment problem from the angle of international labor legislation. One is the regulation of migration and the other the proper distribution of raw material.

Prior to the war, overproduction was often seen to be a dominant cause of periodical financial crises, entailing distress among the workers in spite of an abundant production of goods. We may find, especially since the war, the opposite phenomenon of underproduction due to scarcity of raw materials, leading similarly to distress and unrest, with the closing down of factories and reduction of working forces. Schemes of insurance and even the adjustment of public works in order to provide work in slack seasons will meet the

[1] For a thorough study of the whole problem, see Beveridge, *Unemployment: A Problem of Industry*, 3rd edition, 1917.

problem only inadequately if there is failure to bring together the abundance of raw material awaiting human labor on the one hand and the large surplus of labor on the other hand.

In attempting to control either migration or the distribution of raw materials, caution must be exercised because these are economic problems which involve immense political complications. Nevertheless, in the scientific study of the problem of international labor legislation, these are issues which cannot be dodged.[1]

4. *Employment before and after child birth; the scope of maternity protection laws* [2]

The need of protecting women during their maternity period has received recognition in practically all countries although the legal restrictions vary considerably. The employment of women before and after confinement has been found to have direct bearing on the mortality of infants. The legal protection must apply not simply to the mother but also to the child.

As many as twenty-one nations have already enacted laws relating to this matter, the countries being not only those of western Europe but two states of the Australian commonwealth, New Zealand, South Africa, Japan, Argentine, Brazil and four of the United States.[3] Restriction of employment before and after child birth is the general subject of such laws. The period of exclusion of women is from four to twelve weeks before and after the time of confinement. The Spanish law of exclusion of prospective mothers applies to "any kind of work" so long as the work is de-

[1] See the *Provisional Record of the International Labor Conference at Washington*, 1919, pp. 296-297; also ch. vii.

[2] See *Report iii*, pp. 6-15; also appendices iii-iv of the *Report*.

[3] Connecticut, Massachusetts, New York, Vermont.

fined as "manual" labor. The Belgian law, which is next only to the Spanish in its comprehensiveness, covers "mines, commercial establishments, restaurants and offices attached to industrial works, commercial establishments and transport undertakings as well as factories and workshops." The Greek law covers practically as wide a field as the Belgian and the French and American laws are the next widest in scope of application. There are many countries which exclude commercial and other undertakings, applying the law only to industrial establishments. In a large number of countries the laws exclude the small workshops by fixing arbitrary numerical limitation, which may vary from 3 to 16, that is, for example in Norway women in workshops where less than five persons are employed are outside the scope of legal protection. The variations are briefly as follows: South Africa, 3; New South Wales, 4; Norway, 5; Italy, Denmark and Western Australia, 6; Sweden and Germany, 10; Japan, 16.[1] In some other places the law does no define the number of persons employed in any workshop as the limit of legal control but "small shops" are excluded as a matter of usual practice, as in Switzerland.

The period of exclusion from employment for childbirth varies from four to twelve weeks. In Germany and part of Poland six out of eight weeks of exclusion must follow the confinement. A medical certificate is often required for shortening the period of exclusion. In Switzerland six weeks' exclusion can be extended legally to eight if the woman desires it. In Japan the five-week period can be reduced to three upon presentation of medical certificate. Spanish, Italian, Danish and other laws allow similar reduction of the period if the woman is certified to be fit for work.

[1] *Report iv*, p. 8.

During recent years most laws have been so enacted or modified as to safeguard the economic interest of the woman excluded, recognizing that unless this is done, the legal aim of protection of her health is not effectively carried out. The laws have increasingly given recognition to the right to leave work before confinement and to demand reinstatement after the compulsory rest. In France, Spain, Norway, and Sweden the women may leave work without notice and later claim reinstatement. The Spanish law is most radical; it allows the woman to leave work during eight weeks before childbirth and compels the employer in the meantime to keep her place open. Norway allows four and Sweden two weeks under similar circumstances. The protection of the woman as wage-earner is further secured by grant of insurance benefits or allowances payable for the compulsory retirement. This is done in at least twelve countries either by explicit legal provision or through a broad sickness-insurance scheme. The amount given varies. In Australia a woman is given by virtue of the Maternity Allowances Act (1912), £5 for child birth. In Holland the whole amount of her wages is allowed. In Great Britain the amount is rigidly fixed at 30 shillings. In Germany, Norway, Rumania, Czecho-Slovakia, *etc.*, the maternity benefit is the same as the ordinary sickness allowance, which is 50 or 60 *per cent* of the wages. In several countries the maternity benefit is accompanied by free medical attendance or midwifery.

In spite of all these safeguards, a difficulty seems to be experienced everywhere in enforcing the legal provisions.[1] In order to ensure the health of the mother and the child incentive must be given so as to discourage premature return to work and also efforts should be made to provide

[1] *Report iv*, pp. 14-15.

facilities for nursing mothers to feed their infants while at work. The laws of Argentine, Italy, Norway, Spain and Sweden have such provisions and in a few other countries they are being considered. Our problem is to make this policy worldwide.

5. *Women's Night Work; its dangers and its prohibition*[1]

The physical and moral dangers, which the employment of women during the night entails, need not be dwelt upon. This obvious evil was noticed comparatively early. The Berne convention of 1906 which was signed by fourteen countries of Europe, contained a provision to exclude women from employment during the night defined to embrace the hours between 10 p. m. and 5 a. m.[2]

In the United States the employment of women during the hours between 9 or 10 p. m. and 6 a. m. is prohibited in ten states. Japan and India have enacted laws of this nature. The majority of the Australian states and Canadian provinces have also passed like legislation while other countries are "prepared," as their governments announced, to adhere to the Berne Convention.

The problem as it presents itself for international legislation is the extension and application of the convention.

6. *Employment of children; minimum age of admission to work;*[3] *children's night work*[4]

The employment of children in gainful occupations has been an industrial evil of long standing. While at present in most countries the age of 14 is established as the legal age of admission to work, there are still certain countries, where

[1] *Ibid.*, pp. 16-22.

[2] Chapter iii, section 6.

[3] *Ibid.*, pp. 45-50; also appendix viii.

[4] *Ibid.*, pp. 51-56; appendix ix.

children below that age may be employed. *Thirteen* is the minimum age in France, Germany, the Netherlands, Sweden (boys only) and South Australia; *twelve* in Argentine, Brazil, Italy, Japan, Mexico and Portugal; *eleven* in Rumania; *ten* in Spain; and *nine* in India. In Czecho-Slovakia, Greece, the Netherlands, Norway and Sweden and in thirty-six American states children without the certificate of elementary school education are barred from employment.[1] *Fourteen* is the usual minimum in Europe but in Greece (underground work) and Sweden, and in British Columbia and Quebec it is fixed at *fifteen*. In the United States the Revenue Act of 1918[2] sets the minimum age of work in mines and quarries at 16 by levying a tax of 10 per cent of the entire net profits for the taxable year on mines and quarries employing children under that age. In underground or dangerous work, the minimum age is generally higher. In the states of Arizona and Wisconsin and in Bulgaria, Spain and South Africa, for example, the age limit is *eighteen*.

In Poland, Sweden, Czecho-Slovakia, the Netherlands and elsewhere in Europe and in the United States there is a strong move for raising the age limit to at least *fourteen*.[3]

As to the night work of children, this evil has long been recognized. We have already described the sixteen-year age limit inserted in the Berne Convention of 1913, which though never formally ratified was provisionally agreed upon. This has been adopted by sixteen countries,[4] while a higher age limit of 18 is being set up as a standard in Brazil, Great Britain, Denmark, France, Norway, Sweden, Switzer-

[1] *Report iii*, appendix viii, pp. 151-155.

[2] The tax on employment of child labor act; title xii of the Federal Revenue Act of 1918.

[3] *Report iii*, p. 47.

[4] *Report iii*, p. 51.

land and three states of the United States of America. The Netherlands and Poland (a part) has made it 17, while in Italy, Japan and Rumania the age limit is 15. Generally speaking, 14 years is the lowest limit below which no night work is tolerated. In France it is 13, while in a part of Poland and in Denmark for purposes of industrial training the age is set at 15. In Norway and Sweden it is 16. The exceptions allowed are mostly for continuous industries, for industrial processes dealing with materials which are subject to rapid deterioration and for newspaper printing.

It is desirable to bring the lower standards up to the international standard set up at Berne and then in the course of time to extend the scope and application of that standard.

7. *Employment of women and children in unhealthy processes* [1]

The problem of employment in unhealthy processes presents a task " laborious as well as lofty," to use the words of the Organizing Committee's report. It demands " in most instances time for inquiry and experiment." The problem is difficult because the attempt to meet it presupposes comprehensive data as to the nature and extent of industrial diseases which prevail in each country, besides technical knowledge sufficient to interpret the significance of the data.

The statutory definitions of " dangerous " and " unhealthy trades " vary considerably and no uniformity can be found even as to the principles of regulation as they are applied in different countries.[2] Of course certain regulations dealing with more or less elementary matters such as industrial hygiene, are found in every country. They are the general regulations as to the removal of fumes and dust, use of lead, mercury, phosphorus and arsenic in manufacture, total

[1] *Report iii*, pp. 23-45, 56-60, 66-77, 85-151.

[2] *Report iii*, appendix vi, a-b.

or specified exclusion of women from certain trades involving the use of lead, *etc*. The use of white phosphorus in the manufacture of matches has been referred to in a previous chapter and little more needs be said except to emphasize the desirability of the extension of the prohibition. But with regard to other industrial poisons, the vast field is as yet left untouched by international agreement. A careful study of the prohibitive and protective clauses which are contained in the statutes of various countries indicate the need of no small amount of international regulation.[1]

We should perhaps be reminded that the risks of industrial poisons are by no means uniform. The channels of absorption of the poison vary and the safeguards must be provided accordingly. A substance like lead may be absorbed by the nose and other air passages with dust or fumes. Nitro and amido-derivates of benzene and its homologues such as T. N. T. are absorbed through the skin. Such materials as carbon-bisulphide affect the nervous system and certain substances (*e. g.*, tetrachlorethane) affect the metabolism of the body. Colic, anaemia, wrist-drop and other forms of paralysis, convulsions, loss of sight or of mental equilibrium, *etc.*, are not the only severe results of unprotected industrial processes. Deaths have occurred in large numbers. The need of regulation should never be minimized. The British report for 1900-1918, covering "all reported cases of poisoning under the heads of lead, mercury, phosphorus and arsenic together with cases of anthrax and toxic jaundice," is instructive. It shows the decrease of cases in those years as follows:[2]

Men: from 909 with 38 deaths to 184 with 19 deaths (1914: 469 with 34 deaths); boys—from 25 with 3 deaths to 8 with

[1] *Report iii*, appendix vii, A-D.

[2] *Report iii*, p. 37.

no death (1914: 10 with no death); women—from 165 with 7 deaths to 66 with 10 deaths (1914: 26 with 2 deaths); girls—from 29 with no death to 7 with 1 death (1914: 5 with no death).

An even more striking example is furnished by the following figures of cases of lead poisoning:

Men—from 862 with 30 deaths to 123 with 11 deaths (1914: 415 with 28 deaths); boys—from 21 with 3 deaths to 1 with no death (1914: 4 with no death); women—from 150 with 5 deaths to 20 with 1 death); girls—from 24 with no death to 1 with no death).

In the pottery-industry which involves a large amount of dangerous lead processes:

Men—from 86 with 4 deaths to 5 with no death (1914: 19 with 5 deaths); boys—from 9 with no death to 0 (1914: 1 with no death); women—from 93 with 4 deaths to 6 with no death (1914: 7 with 1 death); girls—from 12 with no death to 0 (1914: 0).

The account given so far only suggests the complexity and vital importance of the problem of the so-called "dangerous," "noxious" and "unhealthy" trades. In order to solve the problem, the regulation, whether national or international, must be preceded by thorough and competent scientific investigation. The nature and extent of the danger must be ascertained; the "poisonous" substances used in manufacturing must be discovered and tabulated after careful study, and recourse must be taken to either total prohibition or restriction of their use. As preventive measures periodical medical examination as well as examination on certain specific occasions should be given. Mechanical draft and exhaust ventilation in connection with crushing and grinding machinery should be enforced unless a "wet" process is applicable. Washing accommodations including baths are indispensable. Protective clothing should be furnished, cloak rooms and mess rooms should be under sanitary control and finally construction of the building, proper ventilation, sufficient light, ample air space and accommodation for cleansing purposes should be required. Adequate medical appliances should be placed in all establishments. Before excluding any class of workers either according to age or sex, it should be remembered that oftentimes a little care will remove the danger of the poison and obviate the need of depriving the worker of his or her opportunity to work.

PART III

AN ATTEMPT AT SOLUTION OF THE DIFFICULTIES IN INTERNATIONAL LABOR LEGISLATION

CHAPTER VII

THE WASHINGTON CONFERENCE OF 1919[1]

1. *Preliminary steps;*[2] *Organizing Committee; action of the U. S.*

SHORTLY after the plenary session of the Paris Peace Conference on April 11, 1919, the "Organizing Committee" for the International Labor Conference to be held at Washington, was appointed as provided for in the Annex to the Labor Section of the Peace Treaty. The appointment was in accordance with the resolution adopted on April 11, by the Plenary Sitting of the Peace Conference. The text of the resolution is as follows:

That the Conference approves the Draft Convention creating a permanent organization for the promotion of the international regulation of labor conditions which has been submitted by the Labour Commission, with the amendments proposed by the British Delegation; instructs the Secretariat to request the Governments concerned to nominate forthwith their representa-

[1] For brief accounts of the conference, see (1) editorial in *London Nation*, Dec., 1919; (2) *Monthly Labor Review, U. S. Bureau of Labor Statistics*, Jan., 1920; (3) Article in *New Republic*, Dec. 24, 1919, by Arthur Sweetzer; (4) Article in *American Federationist*, Jan., 1920 (by Earnest H. Greenwood, Deputy Secretary General of the Conference); (5) Comment in *American Federationist*, Feb., 1920, by an English writer; (6) *The Survey*, Nov. 15, 1919, pp. 107-108; (7) *American Labor Legislaton Review*, Dec., 1919; (8) *La Revue de Paris*, Feb. 15, 1920.

[2] *Cf.* (1) *The League of Nations*, vol. ii, no. 5, published by the World Peace Foundation, pp. 338-342; (2) *Reports i-iii* of the Organizing Committee; (3) *The American Labor Legislation Review*, August, 1919.

tives on the Organizing Committee for the October Conference, and authorizes that Committee to proceed at once with its work.[1]

The members of the Committee were as follows;

United States of America—Dr. J. T. Shotwell (provisionally), Professor, Columbia University.

Great Britain—Sir Malcolm Delevigne, K.C.B., Assistant Under-Secretary of State, Home Office.

France—M. Arthur Fontaine, Counsellor of State, Director of Labor.

Italy—Sig. Di Palma Castilione, Inspector of Emigration.

Japan—Dr. Minoru Oka, formerly Director of Commerce and Industrial Affairs, Ministry of Agriculture and Commerce.

Belgium—M. Ernest Mahaim, Professor at Liège University.

Switzerland — M. W. E. Rappard (provisionally), Professor, Geneva University.

The Committee began its work without delay. Arthur Fontaine was elected chairman and H. B. Butler of Great Britain was appointed secretary. Hardly a month had elapsed after its formation when the Committee addressed a circular, dated May 10, to the governments of the various countries enclosing a questionnaire respecting the agenda of the Washington Conference.

As explained in this circular, the questionnaire "aimed at obtaining the most complete information available in regard to the existing legislation and practice in the different countries in respect to the subjects referred to in the various

[1] *Cf. League of Nations Report i*, prepared by the Organizing Committee for the International Labor Conference, Washington, 1919, prefatory note, p. iii.

items of the agenda, and the proposals of the respective Governments as to how they should be dealt with by the Conference." [1] The circular further described the preliminary business of the conference, the details as to the appointment of delegates and advisors and the manner in which the expenses of the delegates participating in the conference were to be met. Replies were received from twenty-seven countries in time for collating and tabulating the answers. The governments of Argentina, Greece, Guatemala, India, Japan, Nicaragua, Panama and Peru failed to send replies before the Reports, as compiled by the Committee, went to the press.[2]

The results of the Committee's painstaking work of compilation appeared on August 18 in the form of three " Reports ". The first dealt with the question of the hours of work, the second with unemployment and the third with the employment of women and children, as well as with the use of white phosphorus in the manufacture of matches. A compilation of the replies received later from the eight governments mentioned above appeared on September 27 as Report IV,—*Supplemental Report on Certain Countries.*

In the meantime the Congress of the United States, anticipating the Conference, passed on August 2, 1919, a joint resolution[3]—" to authorize the President to convene a meeting of an International Labor Conference in Washington, D. C." The text of the resolution explains the absence of United States' delegates from the Conference, although there was a large representation from countries non-signatory to the League of Nations Covenant. The resolution reads:

Resolved, . . . That the President of the United States be,

[1] See *Report i*, p. 149; *League of Nations*, vol. ii, no. 5, p. 339.

[2] See *Report i*, p. 156 and *Report iv*, pp. 3, 39.

[3] *American Labor Legislation Review*, September, 1919, p. 301.

and he hereby is, authorized to convene and to make arrangements for the organization of a general international labor conference, to be held in Washington, D. C.: *Provided, however*, That nothing herein shall be held to authorize the President to appoint any delegates to represent the United States of America at such conference or to authorize the United States of America at such conference to participate therein unless and until the Senate shall have ratified the provisions of the proposed treaty of peace with Germany with reference to a general international labor conference.

Consequently on August 11, an official invitation was cabled by the President of the United States to 34 countries, for representation at the first official annual meeting of the International Labor Conference, "to assemble in Washington at noon on the 29th day of October, 1919."

2. *Concurrence of International Congresses*

The proposed meeting of the International Labor Conference under the League of Nations led to the calling of an International Federation of Trades Union Congress, to meet in Washington at about the same time. In addition, the first International Congress of Working Women was convoked by the National Women's Trade Union League of America to meet simultaneously.[1] The American Federation of Labor had also planned to hold its conference in the same city within a few weeks. A Washington paper[2]

[1] The call for the first International Congress of Working Women was issued on August 5, 1919, signed by Mary Anderson, the Director of the Women's Bureau of the U. S. Department of Labor and by Mrs. Raymond Robins the President of the Women's Trade Union League of America. The call was sent to 34 countries. For the stand that women workers had taken in regard to the labor section of the Peace Treaty, see "Women Workers and Labor Clauses in the Peace Treaty" in the *Labor Legislation Review*, Sept., 1919, pp. 339-341.

[2] *The Washington Post*, October 28, 1919.

described the city as the "World's Labor Forum," and this description was soon proven to be no exaggeration.

The atmosphere in which these international labor congresses met was, however, hardly congenial to the spirit they embodied.[1] The industrial condition of the country was one of suspense and unrest. A large number of steel workers were out on strike [2] and there was pending still another colossal strike almost unequaled in its magnitude, involving well-nigh half a million workers.[3] There were sinister forbodings that the "coal famine" which would result from the strike might soon paralyze the industry and transportation of the entire nation. The President, whose strenuous efforts on behalf of the Peace Treaty had made him an invalid, called, from his sick-bed, a national council to settle the industrial disputes within the nation.[4] But the council soon proved an utter failure, provoking the anger and hostility of labor and even widening the gap which separates labor from capital.[4] In short, America in the fall

[1] Speaking of the Labor section of the Peace Treaty, Senator James A. Reed said: "and yet sir, it is the most dangerous, and the most revolutionary, the most dangerous, and the most infamous of all the dangerous and infamous provisions of this document which proposes to change the form and structure of the American government and to betray the rights of the American people!" *Cf. Congressional Record,* 66th Congress, First Seession, pp. 8137-8145, 8265, 8269, 8425-8435, *etc.*

[2] See *Senate Report,* no. 289: "Investigating Strike in Steel Industries," also "The Closed Shop" by J. A. Fitch, in *The Survey,* November 8, 1919, pp. 53-57, for the other side of the story.

[3] See "The Coal Strike," by W. L. Chenery in *The Survey,* Nov. 22, 1919, pp. 150-155.

[4] See *The Survey,* "The President's Industrial Conference" by W. L. Chenery, October 25, 1919, pp. 35-37.

[5] Soon after the collapse of the council, Samuel Gompers wrote ". . In effect they laid down the proposition that no gains for human freedom shall be made except through struggle. *To such a challenge there is and ever has been but one answer. The fight must go on. The weapons must be determined by the character of the struggle.*" See *American Federationist,* Dec. 1919, pp. 1121-1125.

of 1919 was suffering from an acute attack of the industrial malady.

3. *Proceedings of the International Congress of Working Women*[1]

This Congress met from October 28 to November 6, and was attended by representatives from more than twenty countries. It was presided over by Mrs. Raymond Robins, the President of the Women's Trade Union League. The Congress labored mainly on the agenda of the League of Nations' Labor Conference, and finally adopted a number of resolutions which were immediately submitted to the Conference for its consideration.[2] The resolutions failed to receive much attention at the hands of the Conference,[3] but they propose standards which are much to be desired and which will be fought for by the women labor leaders at all future conferences till they are attained.

In its resolutions, the International Congress of Working Women requested[4] the first International Labor Conference of the League of Nations to amend article 3 (*i. e.*, article 389 of the Peace Treaty) of the Labor section, concerning the representation of each country at the International Labor Conference, to read as follows:

The Conference shall be composed of six representatives of

[1] See "The Impressions of the Women's International Conference" in *Life and Labor*, the organ of the Women's Trade Union League, Jan., 1920.

[2] Mimeograph record of the proceedings, from the third to the eighth day, contains the discussions and resolutions. The proceedings have not been printed. Only the resolutions are available in printed form.

[3] See *Provisional Record of the International Labor Conference*, p. 41, 5th day, Nov. 4, 1919.

[4] See *Resolutions adopted by First Int. Cong. of Working Women*, p. 2.

each of the high contracting parties; *viz.*: Two delegates representing the Government, one of whom shall be a woman; two delegates representing labor, one of whom shall be a woman; two delegates representing the employers.

In the course of less than a week, the Congress of Working Women acted on each item of the agenda of the League of Nations' Labor Conference and passed appropriate resolutions.

On the first item of the agenda, *i. e.*, the application of the limitation of hours of work to 8 in a day and 48 in a week, the Congress recommended "for all workers a maximum 8-hour day and 44-hour week." It further recommended "an uninterrupted duration of at least one day and a half for the weekly rest period" and "in continuous industries a minimum rest period of one-half hour . . . in each eight-hour shift."

As to the second item (*i. e.*, on unemployment) the Congress expressed the opnion that the nature of the problem was such that it could not be viewed "in isolation from wage standards as a whole nor separated from the social and industrial organizations at present prevailing in all industries," and that the "causes of unemployment have been obscured and remedies obstructed by lack of adequate governmental and international research and control." The Congress recommended the establishment of a special Bureau of Employment in the International Labor Office to act as the International Bureau of Information. It recommended further that a free employment service be established in all cities and industrial towns in the nation. In addition, the resolutions urged the furthering of the system of unemployment insurance, adjustment of public contracts in such a way as to minimize protracted periods of unemployment, suppression of the propaganda of misrepresentation to induce foreign labor to migrate which is being carried on by transportation companies, appointment of women as directors of departments relating specially to women, *etc.*

On the question of maternity insurance, the Congress was not unanimous in its opinion, but it did agree that the employment of women six weeks before and six weeks after child-birth should be prohibited. The majority declared that every woman should be entitled during maternity to free medical, surgical and nursing care, either in a hospital or at home, and also to a monetary allowance. The delegates from five nations [1] resolved to have the clause read: " Every wage-earning woman or the wife of a wage-earner shall . . ." *etc.* The majority also demanded that the monetary allowance given to mothers should be adequate for the full and healthy maintenance of mother and child during the aforesaid period, but the minority [2] voted to have it read: " The indemnity given to mothers shall be based on the living wage in the district."

With regard to night work, the congress not only recommended adherence to the Berne Convention of 1906, but also voted to define " night " as consisting of the hours between 9 p. m. and 6 a. m.

The congress fixed on 16 years as the minimum age for the employment of children, but voted that their admission to industrial work was to be granted only upon the fulfilment of two qualifications besides age; *viz.*, completion of elementary school education and physical fitness. Eighteen years was set up as the minimum age at which children should be admitted to mines or quarries. The congress further demanded a shorter work-day for children between 16 and 18 than the legal work-day for adults. The hours between 6 p. m. and 7 a. m. were defined as " night ", when

[1] Belgium, Czecho-Slovakia, Poland, Italy, Canada.

[2] Belgium, Czecho-Slovakia, Poland, Italy.

children should not be employed. The employment of children in unhealthy processes was to be prohibited. Besides minute provisions for the administration of these regulations, the congress recommended compulsory continuation schools for minors under the age of 18.

With regard to hazardous occupations for women, the congress recommended, among other things, the "prohibition of home work in occupations involving the use of poisonous material," "no exception of small factories from the regulations" and "prohibition of employment of women *only in trades which cannot be made healthy* for women as potential mothers."

In addition to these, which related exclusively to the agenda of the League of Nations' Labor Conference, the congress passed four series of resolutions on Immigration, Distribution of Raw Materials, the Russian situation, and the location of a permanent labor bureau. Claiming that "emigration is a direct consequence of unemployment" and that "it is in the highest interests of the workers of all countries that emigration be regulated," the congress demanded "equal rights for the foreign worker and his family as far as social labor legislation is concerned," "equal wages for foreign and native born workers," and the right of the emigrant nation "to appoint officials to the country to which they emigrate for their assistance and protection."

The congress requested the League of Nations' Labor Conference "to ask the League of Nations to appoint a Committee to consider and plan for the equal distribution of the raw materials existing in the world, as well as the international control of maritime transports which determine the increase of price of the raw materials."

A protest was registered by the congress against the blockade of Russia on the ground that it was "in effect directed against millions of women and children" and had "brought in its train starvation, disease and death to countless victims," and demanded "the removal of all restrictions upon the shipment of food and other necessities to the people of Russia."

Finally, the congress resolved to locate the office of the International Congress of Working Women, in the United States.

4. *The opening session;*[1] *the personnel of the delegation*

On October 29, 1919, at 10 a. m., the first official International Labor Conference met in the Pan-American Building, Washington. On account of the illness of President Wilson, the conference was called to order by Hon. William B. Wilson, Secretary of Labor. In his opening address, Secretary Wilson pointed out that from the days of Moses, the adjustment of the relationship between the employer and the employee, and "securing the acme of production while safeguarding those who toil, and the equitable distribution of that which has been produced, have been ever-present questions." The Secretary then emphasized that universal justice and harmony could not be achieved over night; that only slow and gradual experimentation with due consideration not only to the material comfort but also to the spiritual nature of man were adequate to solve the age-long problems. A sound guiding principle for all deliberative assemblies of this kind was pointed out to the conference when he sounded a warning against all who would "destroy the basis of the structure of modern civilization, the democratic institutions that exist in numerous nations of the world; for after all, of what avail the plow, the sail, or light or land or life, if freedom fail?"[2]

[1] *Provisional Record of the International Labor Conference*, Oct. 29, 1919, first day, pp. 1-14. "The Provisional Record" was published daily in English, French and Spanish during the conference.

[2] *Ibid.*, p. 2.

Secretary Wilson was followed by Mr. John Barrett, the Director General of the Pan-American Union, who on behalf of that great organization welcomed the delegates. The session was closed with the address[1] delivered by the representative of the Italian delegation, Baron Mayor des Planches, who expressed the appreciation of the delegates to the American Government for offering hospitality to the conference and for assembling the delegates " in this beautiful Capitol whose name recalls one of the greatest men who have honored humanity."

The personnel of the delegates is of interest and is worthy of close observation.[2] The government delegates were more numerous than the combined employers' and workers' delegates.[3] This fact can be partially explained by referring to article 389 (= article 3 of the Labor section, Part XIII) of the Peace Treaty, providing that each country is entitled to four delegates but providing further that each member shall " nominate non-Government Delegates and advisors *chosen in agreement with the industrial organizations, if such organizations exist. . . .*"

While this clause should not be construed to imply that the countries without industrial organizations were entitled to no " non-Government Delegates," it resulted in having the full number of representatives chosen and sent almost solely by those countries where industrial conditions were developed to the extent of having both capital and labor

[1] *Ibid.*, p. 3.

[2] *Ibid.*, p. 1; also *Delegates' Official Guide, International Labor Conference*, published in English and French, pp. 7-26.

[3] According to the official report on the first day, the delegates and their advisors *expected* to arrive were as follows: Governments' delegates, 56, advisors, 51; employers' delegates, 24, advisors, 21; employees' delegates, 24; advisors, 43. But this expectation fell short very much to the disadvantage of the workers' side. See *Prov. Rec.*, p. 9.

organized.[1] Many countries which were not signatory to the Peace Treaty made little or no attempt to send delegates to participate fully in the conference. In such cases only the diplomatic agents stationed in Washington were appointed to represent such governments, with the result that no special representatives either of the employers or of the workers[2] were present from these countries.

The absence of United States' delegates was regrettable. The U. S. Chamber of Commerce did not accept the invitation to send a delegate which was extended. The American Federation of Labor was represented by Mr. Gompers in person a few times, but unofficially and without a vote. Due to the restrictions imposed by the resolution[3] of the U. S. Congress, the government of the United States could not participate in any manner. But unofficially, the United States was represented by the presence of the Secretary of Labor, who was elected President of the Conference and who presided in that capacity throughout the entire session. Out of more than forty countries which were represented at the conference, only a few adhered strictly to the provision of the Peace Treaty which requires that "one at least of the advisors should be a woman" when questions specially affecting women are to be considered. Those countries which had women advisors were: Belgium (2), Canada (1), Czecho-Slovakia (1), France (1), Great Britain (3), Italy (1), Japan (1), Netherlands (2), Norway

[1] Probably those governments were "wise" which did not assume the responsibility of appointing delegates who could be challenged as not being really representative of either employers or employees.

[2] Those countries were Brazil, Chili, China, Colombia, Ecuador, Haiti, Nicaragua, Paraguay, Persia, Siam, Uruguay, Venezuela.

[3] Joint Resolution of August 2, 1919. First Session of the 66th Congress.

[4] Article 389 of the Peace Treaty (= article 3 of Part XIII), second paragraph, second sentence.

(1), Poland (1), Serbs, Croats and Slovenes (1), Spain (1), Sweden (1).

5. *The question of admission of German and Austrian delegates*

Whether or not the delegates from the enemy countries, including Germany and Austria, should be admitted to this Conference was a question pending since the Paris Peace Conference. On May 15, 1919, George N. Barnes, the chairman, convened the labor committee, in order to examine the note of the German delegation on the peace conditions.[1] The labor committee then adopted unanimously the letter which was suggested by Mr. Barnes as the reply to the German note to the supreme council. This letter stated that the answer of the committee on the question of the admission of Germany was " in the affirmative," that " if the Germans are to be kept out of the league for any considerable time, the committee thinks that they should be admitted earlier to the labor organization." The committee, however, gave several reasons for suggesting that the admission should be granted immediately *after* and *not* before the Washington Conference.

This suggestion of the labor committee was adopted by the Council of the principal Allied and Associated Powers, which at its sitting on May 17 decided to give effect to the proposal. However, the communications between the Secretary General of the Peace Conference, Mr. Dutasta, and Mr. Barnes, and those between Mr. Dutasta and Mr. Arthur Fontaine in May and August respectively, indicate a development in a different direction from the above stated decision. It appears that Arthur Fontaine held that in

[1]See *Prov. Rec.*, pp. 5-6; 8-9, "The Report of the Organizing Committee," by Arthur Fontaine, Second Session of the Conference, Oct. 29, 1919.

order to allow the admission of Germany *after* and *not before* the Conference it was necessary to go into the cumbrous task of modifying article 387 of the Peace Treaty.[1] The matter was of special importance because it came up immediately before the signing of the Peace Treaty. In the meantime there was an urgent demand voiced by the Italian delegation that the Austrian delegates should be admitted to the Washington Conference. As time went on other complications arose. Even as late as September 6, when the Commission on International Labor Legislation met, no decision could be made.

Finally, on September 11, the Supreme Council took up the matter and adopted a compromise resolution which read in part as follows:

> . . . the question of the admission of German and Austrian delegates to the forthcoming labor congress at Washington should be left to the decision of that Congress. In the meantime, the allied and associated Governments would put no obstacles in the way of the German or Austrian delegates desirous of proceeding to Washington in anticipation of a decision in their favor.[2]

Consequently this question had to be disposed of before the conference undertook its main task of legislative deliberation.

On the second day of the conference, the question of admission of the Germans was introduced. M. Guerin, the French employers' delegate who led the employers' party throughout the conference, stressed the fact that the French delegation had expected before leaving Paris that the Ger-

[1] Article 387 (= article 1, section 1, pt. xiii), reads in part "The original members of the League of Nations shall be original members of this organization and hereinafter membership of the League of Nations shall carry with it membership of the said organization."

[2] *Ibid.*, p. 9.

mans were to be admitted to the conference only after the session. He pointed out that the idea of the Supreme Council was the same. In opposition to the admittance of the Germans, he said:

> . . . Nor is it my intention to be chauvinistic, but distinction should be made between the nations that have acted towards us as barbarians and those who have only defended their rights. Let me call your attention to the fact that the treaty has not been ratified by America and fighting is still going on in certain regions. This is a question of national dignity and justice. It is important that the nation that has treated international covenants as "scraps of paper" should not be on a par with nations which respect international treaties. Let us not forget the unprecedented barbarous manner in which the neutrality of Belgium was violated and the barbarous methods introduced by Germany into warfare! [1]

The view of the employers' representative was opposed boldly by M. Jouhaux, Secretary General of the *Confédération Générale du Travail,* and compatriot of M. Guerin. He said in part:

> We hope that a new era is coming, in which justice will reign and this ideal point must be considered over and above economic conditions. It is necessary that now at the opening of the deliberations of the International Labor Conference, Germany and Austria be immediately admitted. . . . Our present decision is of capital importance to the whole world. . . . My appeal is to the spirit prevailing among the working classes of the allied and associated powers and in their name I appeal to this assembly and propose to you that you adopt the proposal of the Organizing Committee in favor of the immediate admission of Germany and Austria.[2]

[1] Free translation, see pp. 17 and 23, of the *Provisional Record,* 2nd day, Oct. 30, 1919.

[2] *Ibid.*

Before the proposition was finally submitted to vote, M. Carlier of the Belgian delegation, explaining the sentiments of the Belgian delegation, said:

> They [the Belgian delegation] do not wish to vote against it for economic reasons, the necessity of which is clear to everybody, but neither do they want to vote for the motion because Germany has cynically violated all her engagements toward Belgium, and because Germans—that is all the Germans—have systematically and diabolically prosecuted, during the four years of their occupation, the destruction of our entire industry.[1]

After the discussion had lasted for several hours the question was put to vote. Seventy-one were in favor, one (Guerin) against and one (Carlier) abstained from voting. Thus the question was settled with the adoption of the recommendation of the organizing committee "that in anticipation of their admission to the League of Nations and in view of their expressed willingness to coöperate in the work of the labor organization, Germany and Austria are hereby admitted to membership in the international labor organization with the same rights and obligations possessed by the other members of the labor organization."

The German and Austrian delegates, according to their official reports, had already been appointed and the Germans soon started on their way.[2] However, because of the difficulty of obtaining passage on the boats of either the allies or the neutrals, and owing, moreover, to the unexpected brevity of the conference, the German and Austrian delegates did not come to the United States.

[1] *Prov. Rec.*, p. 18.

[2] For the official German and Austrian correspondence, see *Prov. Rec.*, p. 41, 5th day, Nov. 4, 1919; also p. 162, 11th day, Nov. 13, 1919; p. 185, 12th day, Nov. 17, 1919.

6. *The organization of the Conference; the officers; the Committee of Selection*[1]

On the third day of the Conference, October 31, 1919, steps were begun for the permanent organization of the conference. Secretary Wilson was elected President. Three Vice-Presidents were chosen, consisting of George N. Barnes for the Government delegates, Jules Carlier of Belgium for the Employers' delegates, and Leon Jouhaux of France for the workers' representatives. H. B. Butler of Great Britain was chosen Secretary General.

A governing body for the conference, known as the "Committee of Selection" was thereupon formed, comprised of representatives of the three groups as follows:

Government:—Great Britain, Sir Malcolm Delevigne; France, Arthur Fontaine; Japan, Dr. M. Oka; Italy, Dr. Palma Castilione; Belgium, Prof. E. Mahaim; Argentina, Dr. Felipe Espil; Denwark, Dr. S. Neuman; Canada, Senator G. D. Robertson; Czecho-Slovakia, Charles Spinka; Spain, Dr. A. Posada; Switzerland, Dr. Hans Sulzer.

Employers:— Great Britain, D. S. Marjoribanks; France, Louis Guérin; Italy, Ferdinando Quarteri; Japan, Sanji Muto; Spain, A. Sala; Czecho-Slovakia, Francis Hodacz.

Workers:—Great Britain, C. Stuart-Bunning; France, Leon Jouhaux; Belgium, Corneille Mertens; the Netherlands, J. Oudegeest; Spain. Francisco Cabellera; Sweden, H. Lindquist.

Subject to the official staff of the conference a "Secretariat" to transact sundry official business was formed. This body was under the Secretary General, H. R. Butler of Great Britain. He was assisted by Deputy Secretary General H. B. Greenwood of the United States, Dr. G. Pardo of Italy and Chief Assistant Secretary E. J. Phelan

[1] *Prov. Rec.*, 3rd day, pp. 29-31.

of Great Britain together with eight assistant secretaries from the United States, Great Britain, France, Japan and Canada.

In due course, in view of the magnitude of the problems of the conference which obviously could not be settled by speech-making in the plenary session however prolonged, a number of committees were appointed by the governing body. These committees were: (1) Committee on Credentials, consisting of three members; (2) Committee on Unhealthy processes, consisting of twenty-one members representing twelve countries; (3) Committee on Employment of Women, twelve members from twelve different countries; (4) Committee on Standing Orders, nine members from nine countries; (5) Committee on Hours of Work, fifteen members, seven countries; (6) Committee on Applications for Admission, six members, five countries; (7) Committee on Unemployment, thirty one members, fifteen countries; (8) Committee on Tropical Countries, twenty one members, twelve countries.[1]

Some of these committees, were divided into sub-committees in order to consider various phases of the problem which was submitted to the main committee for study and report. These committees met separately. They held at least ten, or more sessions, during which the problems committed to them were thoroughly thrashed out from various angles.

7. *The question of credentials; the cases of France, South Africa, Japan, Cuba and Argentina*

The question of qualification of the delegates to the conference was an "embarrasing" one, to a number of the participating countries.

Article 389[2] of the Peace Treaty provides that "the

[1] See *Prov. Rec.*, 11th day, Nov. 14, 1919, pp. 172-173.

[2] See seventh paragraph, Article 3 of Part xiii, Labor, sec. 1, ch. i.

credentials of Delegates and their advisors shall be subject to scrutiny by the Conference, which may, by two thirds of the votes cast by the Delegates present, refuse to admit any delegate or advisor whom it deems not to have been nominated in accordance with the treaty provisions." In compliance with this article, the Committee on Credentials was appointed, charged with the responsibility of determining the qualifications of delegates who had been challenged. The Committee consisted of Sir Malcolm Delevigne of Great Britain, chairman, representing the government, Jules Carlier of Belgium representing the employers and Jean Oudegeest of the Netherlands representing the workers.[1]

Due to the absence from the Peace Treaty, of any specification as to the form of the credentials, the committee was confronted with the difficulty of determining the validity of the credentials which were submitted in diverse forms, "some giving precise information as to the industrial organization of employers and workers consulted in regard to the appointment of non-government delegates, others giving no such information." [2]

Protests against the appointment of non-government delegates came from France, South Africa, Japan, Cuba and Argentina. The qualification of the French labor delegate was challenged by the French Confederation of Christian Workers on the ground that the French labor delegation was selected solely from the *Confédération Générale du Travail* and included none who were unaffiliated with that organization. In this case the Committee accepted the explanation of the French minister, giving weight to the statement that

[1] See *International Labor Conference Manual*, published by the Japanese Delegation, November, 1919, Washington, pp. 68-77; also *Provisional Record*, pp. 198-203.

[2] See *Prov. Rec.*, pp. 83-84.

the *Confédération Générale du Travail* had a membership of at least 1,300,000 whereas the Confederation of Christian Workers had hardly 75,000 members. The committee recommended "that no action be taken on the protest."

The case of the Japanese labor delegate will be treated in the next chapter.

The challenge against the qualification of the South African delegation was laid before the committee in the form of a letter addressed to the conference by the National Union of Railway and Harbor Services of Cape Town. The complaint was based on the fact that this Union had not been consulted in the appointment of the labor delegate. However, according to the explanation of the official delegates from South Africa, the government had consulted with the South African Federation of Trades which has a membership of 43,000 including the mine workers' union, the society of carpenters and joiners, the society of engineers, the building workers, *etc.* Comparing the total membership of unions unaffiliated with the Federation with the membership of the Federation, the government of South Africa could not be indicted as having failed to conform with the Treaty provisions. The committee's report stated that it could "find no sufficient ground for questioning the appointment of the labor delegate for South Africa." No action was taken on the protest.

The case of the Cuban delegate was comparatively simple. It was raised by the President of the Cuban Federation of Labor Employers' Association, who alleged, without giving particulars, that the Cuban government prevented the federation from appointing a delegate by official interference. This allegation was contradicted by the official delegates from Cuba, who stated that the appointment was made after consultation with the associations of employers in Cuba, including the sugar, tobacco, railway and shipping industries, and that the Employers' Federation was invited to participate in the conference. The committee decided that the government of Cuba had not necessarily disregarded the Treaty provisions in choosing the employers' delegate and therefore it was recommended that no action be taken on the protest.

At the time that the Committee on Credentials made its first report of findings,[1] the Argentine delegation had not yet arrived and that made it impossible for the committee to pass judgment upon the protest that had been raised against the labor delegate from Argentina. As soon as the delegation arrived, the qualification of the labor delegate was subjected to the scrutiny of the committee and the findings were reported to the plenary sitting.[2] This was a case of much greater gravity than the former in that the protest was lodged by the International Federation of Trades Union and the objection was raised in the name of that organization. The letter of protest was addressed to the Committee on Credentials, signed by W. A. Appelton, President; L. Jouhaux, First Vice-President; C. Mertens, Second Vice-President; and J. Oudegeest, Secretary. The situation was as follows: The labor delegate was selected by the Argentine government from the association known as La Fraternidad, which is the oldest union in Argentina, being an organization of railway workers, with a membership of 15,000. There is another labor organization known as the Argentina Federation of Trade Unions, which claims to have a membership of 80,000, affiliated with the International Federation of Trades Union. The government delegate from Argentina stated that the Federation's membership fluctuated considerably from time to time and its present membership was probably between 20,000 and 30,000.

[1] Nov. 6, 1919, eighth session of the conference.

[2] *Prov. Rec.*, p. 198; also pp. 267-270.

The contention of the International Federation was that the Federation of Trade Unions had a larger membership than La Fraternidad, hence was more representative and ought to have been consulted. Upon this ground, Jean Oudegeest dissented from the decision of the majority of the Committee and held, as he had done in the letter of protest, that the Argentine labor delegate should be barred from the conference. The majority of the Committee admitted the claims of the Argentine government that La Fraternidad was a " labor union in conformity with the Argentine law," that "it was the oldest organization," that it was "the only association which represented workers in all parts of the country and which is recognized by and has any responsibilities under the law of the State," and finally that there was " no question as to the delegate being a *bona-fide* representative of the workers so far as the railway industry was concerned."

The problem was understood by every delegate to be of serious moment. Impassioned speeches were made and after more than three hours' debate, the report was put to a record vote. The motion of Oudegeest, to debar the Argentine delegate was defeated by a vote of 44 to 25.

8. *Admission of countries non-signatory to the Peace Treaty*

This question had originally been referred by the conference to the Commission on Applications for Admission. The principal countries under consideration were Finland, Luxembourg, Dominican Republic and Mexico. The International Labor Conference represents the governments officially and membership in it can only be granted on application from the government of a nation. Therefore the committee had no difficulty in deciding upon the cases of Luxembourg, Dominican Republic and Mexico, countries whose governments had not at that time sent in their applications directly. A unanimous report of the committee (no III) [1] stated:

Decisions taken by the conference will impose some obligation, at least morally, on the States members of the Organization. It is therefore the States, through their governments, and not individual organizations of employers and workers which become members of the International Labor Organization. It is therefore important that applications should be entertained only if they are submitted in due form by the government concerned.

Difference of opinion developed on the question of the admission of Finland to membership and the report of the commission was divided.[2] The majority report, presented by Gino Baldesi was in favor of admission, on the broad basis of principle. The minority report, presented by Mr. Rowell, President of Privy Council of Canada was against admission. The minority held that the Supreme Council had no right to interpret the treaty, and that admission to the international labor organization was a question whose solution was under the jurisdiction of the League of Nations. Upon this ground, Mr. Rowell moved that the conference recommend to the League of Nations the immediate admission of Finland and in the meantime to grant the delegates informal participation in the Conference. The contention of Mr. Baldesi was that Germany and Austria presented an analogous case to that of Finland and that as the case of Germany and Austria had been referred to the

[1] See Appendix, pp. 142-143 to the *Provisional Record*, Nov. 12, 1919; see also p. 313, 16th day, Nov. 24, 1919. Luxembourg was admitted then on the same condition as Finland as soon as request for admission was telegraphed by the minister of State of Luxembourg to the conference. The vote was unanimous.

[2] See *Prov. Rec.*, pp. 131-139, Nov. 12, 1919.

Conference that of Finland might also be dealt with by it. Now that the former two countries had been admitted, there could be no ground, he thought, for contending that the Peace Treaty (article 387) excluded Finland from participation in the conference. Senator von Koch of Sweden was of the opinion that the power of the Supreme Council to interpret the Peace Treaty ceased when the League of Nations came into existence. He maintained that it was vitally important that a country like Finland which has an advanced industrial state should be admitted to the conference. The Senator's opinion was supported strongly by the representatives of Denmark and Norway, countries which have a close bond of interest as neighbors of Finland. To enable that country to have its laws and conditions brought into accord with the decisions of the conference and to establish a harmonious standard for every country were the ends sought by these delegates. But Sir Malcolm Delevigne arose to support the motion of Mr. Rowell. He considered the legalistic construction of the Treaty provisions as not merely tenable but as all important. He asserted that his opinion represented the judgment of the entire British delegation and that in case Finland were admitted in spite of the objection, the government of Great Britain would fight the case out before the permanent court of international justice.

The situation was so complex that the question of the admission of Finland was discussed for two days. On the second day,[1] the opposing forces again met, the labor delegates favoring admission and the employers' and government delegates siding with the minority which recommended refusal of admission. Stuart-Bunning, the British workers' delegate, then arose and contradicted every word said by

[1] 11th day, Nov. 13, 1919. See *Prov. Rec.*, pp. 157-161.

Sir Malcolm Delevigne. He stated that the opinion of the workers was not at all in agreement with that of the government delegation. He disapproved Sir Malcolm's "threatening words" which were expressed on the preceeding day and he voiced in explicit terms the solidarity of the workers in words and action. Finally, Canada yielded to the opposition and brought in a Compromise Amendment which was accepted by Gino Baldesi and unanimously adopted. It read:

The conference, without giving a ruling on the question of principle, welcomes the delegates nominated by Finland to attend the Washington meeting, and invites these delegates to take part in the conference on the same conditions as obtain in the case of other countries which have not adhered to the covenant of the League of Nations.

9. *The question of Spanish as an official language*

One of the notable issues which was brought up early in the conference was that of making Spanish an official language. It was introduced with no intention apparently of pushing it as an issue of great consequence. However, a little reflection upon that subject makes it clear why it could not be lightly decided. On the first day of the conference, as soon as the French report of the Organizing Committee was rendered into English, Dr. J. C. Garcia, Government delegate from Ecuador, appealed to the conference on behalf of the Spanish-speaking peoples. He modestly requested that the report should be translated into Spanish also. He said there were at least twenty-five delegates who belonged to Spanish-speaking nations and who spoke Spanish. He then pointed out that there were as many as 18 nations represented at the conference, which used Spanish as their official language.

The proposal received the ardent support of the Spanish government delegate Viscount de Eza, in whose opinion this question could not be brushed aside as "a matter of minor importance" as Arthur Fontaine called it. He maintained that there was more than mere courtesy involved in the question. He said: "For the Spanish-speaking delegates this is a question of principle, and on this matter I must absolutely insist on the use of the Spanish language." He drew attention to the fact that the notices put up in the conference hall were in Spanish, French and English. He said that out of courtesy for the present assembly and out of sympathy for the French and English languages he would, in order to avoid difficulties, renounce any further claims but he "would like to have a definite answer as to whether the gentlemen responsible for the matter think that the standing orders will be adopted only at the end of the conference or whether there is any hope that in a few days Spanish will be adopted as one of the official languages." [1]

The issue threatened to precipitate a stormy discussion, but through the tactful management of the President, Secretary Wilson, and of Secretary General Greenwood, who announced that a Spanish text of the daily bulletin would be supplied through the courtesy of the United States government, the question was temporarily withdrawn.

[1] See *Prov. Rec.*, pp. 11-13.

CHAPTER VIII

THE WASHINGTON CONFERENCE (CONTINUED)

1. *Question of the 8-hour day; main convention*

The general discussion on the first item of the agenda, namely, the application of the principle of the 8-hour day or 48-hour week as the limit of industrial work, was commenced on the fifth day of the conference by George N. Barnes who introduced the subject on behalf of the Organizing Committee.[1]

Mr. Barnes' explanation was a lengthy discourse. He emphasized that labor had long ceased to be a mere commodity, that it must be treated " in terms of sentient human beings," that it is entitled to leisure, to live lives outside of the workshops, to time for recreation, for education and for the discharge of social and family duties. He pointed out specifically three or four " general considerations which leap to the mind." In the first place, he said with regard to the draft convention:

It is not a mere basic 8-hour law or 8-hour rule with additional pay for additional hours of work that we are after That would not give us what we want. What we do want is leisure, and we must therefore keep that in mind all the time. We are after leisure rather than pay. Moreover even if we arranged for additional pay to be made to the workers for additional time—inasmuch as wages, after all, tend to certain levels, determined by many things apart from the hours of

[1] Nov. 4, 1919, see *Prov. Rec.*, pp. 41-46; for a brief synopsis of the matter, see *Monthly Labor Review*, Jan., 1920, pp. 8-10.

labor—the additional pay would tend to disappear from the very moment it began to be paid. . . .

Secondly he emphasized that the convention should be so framed as to " make it elastic enough to meet the needs of these men who labor, and at the same time, rigid enough to get something like uniformity in its application. Fire, flood, acts of God of any kind—all these have to be specifically provided for." He pointed out that " administrative authorities differ in efficiency and therefore will be lax here and rigid there " and that therefore no absolutely uniform regulation would be possible. As to the choice between the 8-hour day and 48-hour week, he reminded the conference of the existence of places where Sunday rest is unknown. In those places, if the rigid eight-hour day was enforced, a 56-hour week would result. With regard to the countries where industry is undeveloped, he said: " To bring India or Japan into competition would be simply to destroy their mass of industry, and to try would be to court failure."

He moved then:

That the draft convention on the 48-hour week prepared by the Organizing Committee be adopted by the conference as the basis for discussion, but that the question of its application to the tropical and other countries referred to in the 3rd paragraph of article 405 of the treaty be referred in the first instance for consideration by the special committee which shall report to the conference.

Mr. Barnes argued further that while increased production must be had, it could be hoped for only through a better organization of industry, and by humanizing the conditions of work. Long hours of work would not contribute to that end but would be disastrous to man and to industry instead.

Objection to putting this matter to an immediate vote was raised by the employers' group. A substitute plan was subsequently presented by D. S. Marjoribanks of Great Britain and Jules Carlier of Belgium; but the draft of the amendment was not signed by the Italian, Dutch and Canadian Employers' representatives. The employers were willing to accept the 8-hour day or 48-hour week in "principle," but they proposed to modify the provisions, especially those relating to maintenance of productive work, distribution and reconstruction of industry in the regions devastated by the war.

A comparison of the employers' amendment with the amendment proposed by Leon Jouhaux and seconded by Tom Shaw (British workers' delegate) throws an interesting light on the different attitudes of the capitalist and the working man.[1] The employers would replace the word "convention" by "recommendation" wherever it occurs in the text of the draft convention.[2] They would simplify the list of industries to which the 8-hour limit applies. They would construe the "working hour" to mean "actual working hour" and suggested adding the word "actual." Instead of the words "in case of accident," they suggested the phrase "either for preventing accident or in making good repairs after accident," *etc.*, and thereby they would make it possible to have longer working hours. For overtime to be allowed per year they propose 300 hours instead of the 150 hours, which the original draft provided.

A sweeping demand quite characteristic of the conservative mind of some employers was in the new article which they proposed for addition, which follows:[3]

[1] See Appendices ii and iii, in *Prov. Rec.*, pp. 290-292, 15th day, Nov. 22, 1919.

[2] See *Report i* of the Organizing Committee, pp. 141-146.

[3] See *Prov. Rec.*, p. 291, article 12 (b).

All countries without distinction—With a view to reducing the high cost of living, which is an inevitable consequence of the shortage of products and of the difficulty of distributing them, the conference recommends deferring likewise, for a period not to exceed five years, the enforcement of the 48-hour week in industries whose products are indispensable for food supply and in transport industries. These exceptions shall not be put into effect except by virtue of international agreements emanating from the International Labor Office, as special conditions for a definite length of time terminating with the reëstablishment of normal conditions of production.

The workers' amendment, on the contrary, showed vividly the " impetuous mood " of the workers to extend as widely as practicable the application of the limitation of hours of work. They demanded that the 8-hour convention should apply to " commercial " as well as " industrial " undertakings, and the term " undertakings " was to mean both public and private work and " all branches thereof of whatsoever kind."

Leon Jouhaux was not satisfied with the 48-hour week without explicit guarantee of the 8-hour day. He insisted that " the 8-hour day *and* 48-hour week " should be set up as the maximum. Samuel Gompers,[1] who was granted the privilege of addressing the conference as a guest, claimed that the history of industry amply proved that " there is more produced by the workers, everything else being equal, in an 8-hour day, than in a 10 or 12-hour day."

The argument which lasted for a week generally centered around a few important economic considerations. That the present world was in dire need of increased production and that every tendency to lessen or limit production must be prevented was one appealing argument raised to oppose the limitation of working hours. Louis Guerin reiterated

[1] See *Prov. Rec.*, pp. 60-64, 6th day, Nov. 5, 1919.

that the duty of the worker was to produce. "More production," he asserted, was the "only way to get shorter hours of work." It was remarked in this connection that the introduction of the 8-hour day in France had resulted in the reduction of production by 15 to 20 per cent.[1] Leon Jouhaux, who consistently championed the cause of better labor legislation, insisted on the other hand that if more production is needed, improvement should be made in machinery, management and facilities of production, rather than to lengthen the working hours. He asserted that experience during the war and scientific investigation both had demonstrated that lessening the working hours resulted in increased production. Emphasis was likewise placed on the social and ethical importance of the shorter work-day.

The question was finally referred[2] to the Committee on Hours of Work for close study of the problem *in camera*. The committee consisted of 15 members, each group (government, employers and workers) being represented by 5 delegates. The committee held twelve sessions altogether[3] and the final report on the subject, exclusive of the application of the principle to the tropical and special countries, was made to the plenary session of the conference on November 24, by the chairman of the Committee, Arthur Fontaine.[4]

The task of the committee was to revise the draft convention, which had been prepared by the Organizing Committee, in the light of the opinion of the conference as expressed in the debate. Thus the final report was in the

[1] See *Prov. Rec.*, p. 99, 8th day, Nov. 7, 1919.

[2] See *Prov. Rec.*, p. 119, 9th day, Nov. 10, 1919.

[3] The sessions were not open to the public. Only mimeograph reports, written partly in French and partly in English were available to the writer.

[4] See *Prov. Rec.*, pp. 313-321, 347-352; *etc.*, Nov., 1919.

form of a draft convention which the plenary session should either adopt or reject.[1] In presenting the draft M. Fontaine stated that in the opinion of the committee there were three ways of controlling the application of the principle.

First the application should be controlled by the organizations of employers and workers. Those organizations should be consulted about any changes or exceptions that are to take place. In some cases their previous agreement must be obtained. A second control would be exercised by the international labor office, to which several reports must be submitted, reports about exceptions, the working of the details and others. Finally, the committee believed that several governments would exercise control.

The convention as a whole provides an 8-hour day and 48-hour week for "all industrial undertakings public or private and to all branches thereof of whatsoever kind, other than undertakings in which only members of the family are employed."[2] However, a glance at the convention draft reveals the caution of its authors, as they have allowed far-reaching exceptions in order apparently to permit the applications of the convention on as wide a scale as possible under varying circumstances. Thus the provisions of the convention do not apply to "persons holding positions of supervision or management, or employed in a confidential capacity." Furthermore, it states:[3]

Where by law, custom or agreement between the employers'

[1] See for the full text of the Committee's report, accompanied by the draft convention and the draft prepared by the Organizing Committee, pp. 285-292 of the *Provisional Record*, 15th day, Nov. 22, 1919.

[2] Article 2 of the "Draft Convention limiting the hours of work in industrial undertakings to 8 in the day and 48 in the week."

[3] Article 2, clause (b) of the "Draft Convention limiting the hours of work," see also *Prov. Rec.*, p. 288.

and workers' organizations (or where no such organizations exist, between the employers' and workers' representatives) the hours of work on one or more days of the week are less than eight, the limit of eight hours may be exceeded on the remaining days of the week by the sanction of the competent authority, or by agreement between such organizations or representatives: *Provided, however,* that in no case under the provisions of this paragraph shall the daily limit of eight hours be exceeded by more than one hour.

Obviously this clause provides for the Saturday half holiday, where it is desired, without reducing the weekly limit of forty-eight hours. Where workers are engaged in "shifts," exceptions are provided to allow employment in excess of 8 hours a day or 48 hours a week, provided that the average number of hours over a period of three weeks or less does not exceed 8 per day and 48 per week.[1] Work in excess of such limitations is permitted in case of accident, actual or threatened, or in case of urgent work to be done to machinery or plant or in case of "*force majeure,*" but only when necessary to avoid serious interference with the regular working of the undertaking.[2] A 56-hour week average is set as the maximum allowed in "continuous processes in which work is done by a succession of shifts." Holidays, it is provided further, must not be affected by this limitation of working hours. Overtime pay is set at "time and a quarter" as the minimum.[3] The convention further places obligation on the employer to post conspicious notices in the works stating the conditions of employment fixed for the particular industry or trade. In the event of war or "emergencies endangering the national safety," the government may suspend the provisions of the convention. In

[1] *Ibid.*, article ii, (c).

[2] *Ibid.*, article ii, (c).

[3] *Ibid.*, article vi, (b).

general July 1, 1921, is fixed as the date for the convention going into effect.

The adoption of the convention, with its ingenious devices to hold firm the principle of the 8-hour day and 48-hour week, while giving ample flexibility, was not easily secured. M. Fontaine had hardly resumed his seat when a Canadian delegate arose to oppose the adoption of the draft.[1] His objections to the draft were not altogether pertinent but a close analysis of his nine points of objection reveals certain matters of economic interest which are fundamental.

The delegates from Great Britain, France, Canada, South Africa and others took part in the discussion attempting to rebut his arguments, prolonging the debate for several hours. Mr. Crawford, the young South-African labor delegate proposed, with his usual tone of impulsive energy, that in order to eliminate the evils of sweating in industry, " home-work " should also be included in the convention and be subjected to control.[2] His proposal was imbued with a rather acute sense of dissatisfaction over the draft, which " failed " as he asserted, "to protect the poor worker, the woman worker, the home worker and the children, the sweated workers."

His contention, briefly, was that the explicit exclusion of family work from legal control was in effect an official encouragement of the evil of sweating. He pointed out that the lessening of the hours of work in the well-regulated, sanitary factories, unaccompanied by control of home work, amounted to nothing less than forcing the poor worker to seek employment in his unsanitary home and thus fill up with sweating the leisure time obtained as due result of the convention. The Crawford objection, formulated in

[1] See *Prov. Rec.*, p. 313.

[2] *Ibid.*, pp. 319-320.

the form of an amendment, was finally put to vote but was overwhelmingly defeated.

In the course of the debate, a number of interesting suggestions were brought up. The proposition of the Swiss labor delegate, Mr. Ilg, is of interest.[1] He declared that the conference had been "mistaken" in discussing the 8-hour day and 48-hour week. Said he:

> We ought to have found another basis for our discussion—*an eight hour day and forty-five hour week*, and as we have neglected to treat this subject on this occasion, we should at least make sure that it will be treated at our next conference. Gentlemen, the fight for 45 hour week has already been begun by the workers in several countries. It is impossible, sir, for the International Labor Conference to get around this question and not grapple with it honestly. The principle at least must be recognized!

He then submitted a motion to the effect that the next conference should treat this question as an item of the agenda. This motion received no immediate support, but the fact of his proposal needs to be recorded as indicating the direction in which the conferences of the future will necessarily move.

2. *The problem of the "undeveloped countries"—the case of Japan; her difficulties and claims*

The part that was played by Japan at the Paris Peace Conference, as one of the original "Big Five," was no inconspicuous one. At present Japan holds a seat in the Governing Body of the International Labor Office as one of the eight powers of "chief industrial importance" in the world.[2] The one-time Hermit Kingdom of the mys-

[1] *Ibid.*, p. 321.

[2] *Ibid.*, p. 353. See the official report with list of countries represented on the governing body.

terious Orient is to-day no longer a nation that is simply heard of or discussed through the press. The pressure of this young and ambitious nation, now aspiring to be permanently regarded as the leading power of unawakened Asia, is being felt universally. There is little doubt that this circumstance rendered the dilemma of Japan at this conference conspicuous. Her difficulty was this: A certain enterprising portion of Japan saw her industrial ruin in the proposal of the Washington conference, while the government of Japan, anxious to maintain the position of distinction which had been won in the spheres of politics and diplomacy, would have liked to accept all the modern standards, at least in form. Her much-quoted declaration of industrial policy, that "every effort will be made to accelerate the unqualified adoption of the rule in harmony with the general trend of the world," [1] is found in her answer to the questionnaire of the Organizing Committee. The thinking public of Japan demanded the immediate adoption of such a policy [2] as was then declared, and the far-seeing representatives of the government, such as Dr. Minoru Oka,[3] fully realized that Japan must accept a certain standard of labor somewhat similar, if not wholly equivalent, to that of her sister powers of the Occident, if Japan would show her readiness to assert equality among the powers.

Thus the problem which confronted Japan at this conference was whether to accept the international standard at the risk of industrial ruin, or to beg exemption from the

[1] *International Labor Conference Manual*, p. 84.

[2] See "What Japanese Labor Wants" by S. Kusama in the *Japan Review*, Nov., 1919, pp. 13-15.

[3] Dr. Oka, former Director of Commerce and Industrial Affairs in the Ministry of Commerce and Agriculture, was responsible for drafting and carrying into effect the first Factory Law of Japan which is still in force.

world of advanced legislation in order to secure her industrial foundations. A Washington paper in its headline in large letters wrote: "Japan Balks at 8-hour Day!" . . . "Working class claimed as much inferior to civilized nations," *etc.* In seeking compromise many things had to be admitted. In short, Japan had to face here a "hard choice in the full glare of the limelight of pitiless publicity." [1]

A little observation of the industrial conditions in Japan enables one to comprehend the nature of the dilemma which faced the Japanese delegates at the conference. The growth of industry in Japan is only of recent date. Her industrial expansion has been as sudden and phenomenal as the emergence of the nation itself on the international horizon. In 1900 there were only about 120,000 "factory hands," but in 1919 the number had increased to over 3,000,000. The increase of the number of factories has been even more phenomenal. In 1900 there were only about 1,400 factories but in 1919 there were 30,000.[2] For a number of years Japan had been burdened with financial difficulties. As the result of the Russo-Japanese conflict, on the outbreak of the Great War she had an indebtedness amounting to something like $1,500,000,000. But the Great War altered the situation. The greatest calamity to the rest of the world seemed, temporarily at least, "the golden opportunity of a thousand years" to Japan. With the disappearance of the competition of the European powers, she gained a free hand for trade expansion and commercial enterprise. Financial chaos, extinction of industry and general disaster in Europe spelt prosperity for Japan and suddenly,

[1] Article by Robert T. Small, *The Washington Post*, Tuesday, Nov. 25, 1919, pp. 1-2. See also p. 1 of the issue of Nov. 27, 1919.

[2] These figures are based on the study of G. Spencer, who has spent over 18 years in Japan and who is now engaged in industrial research in the Interchurch World Movement.

from the condition of a debtor nation, she rose to be a creditor nation. Before the war her foreign trade showed a balance practically never in her favor, but with the opening of the war, as a foreign observer puts it, "streams of gold began to flow in." Her pre-war exports showed a total annual value of something like 586,797,000 yen, the figure for 1914, but when the war ended they had risen to over 1,931,000,000 yen [1]—an increase of nearly 400 per cent, and the curve of increase seemed acutely on the rise!

Such a situation, however, caused obviously by the war and other extraordinary circumstances, was, at least in part, abnormal. With the cessation of hostilities and resumption of trade competition by the world on a fiercer scale than ever, Japan knows not what future lies before her. In both quality and quantity, Japanese goods must meet competition in the markets which are reopened to her rivals and she must expect that some of those markets will be closed to her when European industry resumes its full swing. In other words, the financial success and industrial prosperity of Japan, in the eyes of those who observe, may be after all a transient phenomenon.

A glance at the state of industrial regulation in Japan raises further doubts as to the stability of her industry.[2] No law regulating either the hours, wages or conditions of labor was in operation until three years ago. The first Japanese factory law was promulgated on March 28, 1911,[3] but its enforcement was not authorized by Imperial Ordinance until August 2, 1916.[4] An examination of this factory act reveals a number of matters that are found but

[1] See "Exports and Imports, 1910-1918" (*Seizohin-sonota-no-Yushitsniu gaku*) published by Dept. of Agr. and Comm., Japan, pp. 1-8.

[2] See the *International Labor Conference Manual*, pp. 99-147.

[3] Law no. 46.

[4] Imperial Ordinance, no. 193.

rarely in the industrial legislation of to-day. In the first place, it applies only to factories in which more than 15 operatives are regularly employed or "where the business is of a dangerous character or is considered injurious to health."[1] It applies in effect only to women and children, prescribing a maximum work-day of 13 hours. George N. Barnes has summarized the situation ably on the basis of the reports and statements of the Japanese government delegates at the conference.

The law [he said], limits the working day to 13 hours per day and in one industry (raw silk) the largest in the country, 120 hours' overtime is allowed in addition. Moreover, there is no weekly holiday like Sunday and 13 hours is actually worked in the silk industry every day, except 2 each month. That is, on the 1st and 15th of the month there are holidays [but no other]. In other industries the working day nominally is about 10, but actually is about 12, because of the fact that overtime is quite common, and therefore we have this condition of things in Japan: that in the silk industry which employs 900,000[2] work-people, the hours are 13 per day, plus one hour overtime for 120 days in the year. In the cotton industry, the hours are 11.[3]

This statement is in line with the following table, showing the number of factories classified according to normal working hours, including rest time. The table is based on the Factory Inspectors' Annual Report (*Kōjō-Kantoku Nenpō*, 1918-1919) and includes only the factories which come under the Factory Law.

[1] See article 1, i-ii of the Factory Law of 1911.

[2] 53% of this number does not come under the scope of the law.

[3] See *Prov. Rec.*, p. 423, 19th day, Nov. 27, 1919. Compare this with articles 3-8 of the Factory Law of 1911. Also article 3 of Ordinance no. 19 of the Dept. of Agr. and Comm., August 3, 1916.

NUMBER OF FACTORIES CLASSIFIED ACCORDING TO NORMAL WORKING HOURS

(Including rest time: a = one shift; b = two or more shifts)

	8 hrs.		9 hrs.		10 hrs.		11 hrs.		12 hrs.		13 hrs.		14 hrs.	
	a	b	a	b	a	b	a	b	a	b	a	b	a	b
Silk reeling........	4	6	2	..	29	..	77	..	392	2	434	..	1845	..
Spinning....	6	..	1	1	11	5	11	18	75	106	..	..	16	..
Twisting	..	..	..	..	32	1	25	..	132	9	..	..	....	..
Weaving	16	3	71	..	156	6	279	13	2579	226	24	..	287	..
Machine and engineering	10	..	42	..	561	2	244	..	216	17	13	..	25	..
Ship building works and wagon shops.	3	..	8	..	127	2	49	..	25	..	2	..	1	..
Tools and implements	17	..	32	..	314	2	115	..	65	4	10	..	3	..
Metalware works...	46	..	104	..	1857	3	471	3	599	40	34	..	17	..
Ceramics..........	52	6	57	5	403	1	210	3	656	43	3	..	6	..
Paper mills........	3	..	1	1	40	3	46	6	159	94	..	..	....	..
Matches and other combustibles	7	..	14	..	93	3	63	..	56	2	1	..	....	..
Oil and fat works ..	15	2	18	1	64	5	31	1	175	27	1	..	....	..
Chemicals	12	3	32	5	135	15	78	6	138	57	2	..	1	..
Totals	189	14	382	13	3822	49	1699	50	4680	587	534	..	2138	..

3. *The struggle of Japanese labor*

Under such circumstances it was evident that Japan was entitled to some modifications in the convention on the eight-hour day. For, as Mr. Barnes pointed out, "if Japan were to be brought down to the same level as other countries," the conference would be " making Japan reduce her production by about 60% while the other countries were having to reduce theirs probably only by about 5, 10 or

[1] The rest period, which is granted the workers whose normal working time is less than 10 hours per day, is 30 minutes generally. For the workers whose normal working hours exceed 10 hours, a rest period running from 30 to 40 or even 60 minutes is allowed.

In these factories there are many instances of work done for 1 or 2 hours or even 3 or 4 hours after the daily normal working time. Such extra work is done principally by the adult male workers.

15%." [1] However, an adjustment of the draft suitable to Japan was made doubly difficult by the condition in which Japanese labor was placed at home.[2] The laborers were demanding the recognition of labor unions and the repeal of a certain police regulation, which was alleged by them to be repressive, and thus their attitude was not in accord with that of the government even on international labor agreements. There was no greater unanimity of spirit among the Japanese labor and government delegates than there was in other delegations. Here irony had its way; the conference stubbornly asserted its internationalism. The voice of Japanese labor found its sympathetic echo among the representatives of European labor and the labor delegates unitedly opposed any modification of the eight-hour convention for Japan.

How internationalism transcended petty national boundaries at this conference was dramatically shown by the appeal which the Japanese labor delegate made to the labor leaders of other countries in protest against the efforts of the government and employers' delegates to have Japan considered as a "special country." In one of the meetings of the labor delegates, Masumoto, the Japanese labor representative, pleading for the help of his colleagues in the emancipation of Japan's millions of toilers said:

. . . I cherish no misgiving as to the hearty coöperation and sympathy which the labor leaders here assembled would manifest toward the workers of Japan, once they have acquainted themselves with the labor conditions of the latter. Inasmuch as the labor leaders of this conference, moved by sentiments of justice and humanity, are assuming the responsibility of

[1] See *Prov. Rec.*, p. 423; also *Report i* of the Organizing Committee for the extent of the 8-hour day already in practice.

[2] See "Some Social Problems of Present Japan" in the *Japan Review*, Dec., 1919, pp. 54-57.

obtaining fair and humane conditions of labor, I have every reason to believe that the millions of toilers of Japan, will soon gain *by your help* the recognition of the right of association, the protection against unemployment, adequate living wages and the protection of women and children. . . . We need the hearty moral support and intelligent advice of all labor leaders assembled here to-day. The task before us is stupendous. That I will consecrate my whole life to the cause of labor and its welfare is my sincere promise to you. May I count on you to lend me your assistance and coöperation in our work? [1]

The plea was not made in vain. The response of the energetic and militant laborities such as Jouhaux, Mertens, Oudegeest, Baldesi and others came like the attack of the Macedonian phalanx. The entire morning session of November 27th was spent in the controversy over the question of " special treatment " for Japan.[2]

It is generally agreed now that few countries of the world took the International Labor Conference quite as seriously as did Japan. Principally it was the greatly agitated labor conditions in Japan which accounted for this attitude. The abnormality of the war-time industry in Japan brought a flood of gold into the hands of the entrepreneurs, but it precipitated discontent and unrest among the workers. Strikes grew to be common. Toyohiko Kagawa, who has devoted years of his life to social reformation, has recently written that " formerly the nature of the strikes was more or less emotional, but now it is done simply from economic discontent. It shows the danger of the coming class struggle in Japan."[3] According to his figures the number of strikes has increased in the course of

[1] The full text of Masumoto's speech is found in *The Japan Review*, Jan., 1920, pp. 81-82.

[2] See *Prov. Rec.*, pp. 423-432; see also section 4 of this chapter.

[3] See *The Japan Review*, Dec., 1919, p. 55.

five years from the outbreak of the war, more than 730 per cent. In 1914 there were only 50 strikes recorded, but in 1918 there were 417. The number of workers involved has also increased proportionately. In 1914 only 7,904 struck, but in 1918 the figure rose to 66,457. Nevertheless such a rapid spread of agitation and unrest could not be construed to mean that labor was gaining much ground. For years Japanese labor has had little or no freedom of organization. Or at least the right of association which is expressly granted by the constitution has in the case of the workers been so restricted that there could be no " union " labor in the occidental sense of the term. The consensus of liberal opinion in Japan seems to agree on the point that the existence of so-called " article 17 of the Police Regulation " has been a menace to labor. All labor leaders, including Suzuki of Yu-ai Kai, have strenuously and bitterly contended that this " article 17 " is " one of the worst laws of the land," because it has been used as the weapon to crush and prevent the organization of labor.[1] Accordingly it was quite natural that the tidings of the International Labor Conference, to be held in the spirit of the nine principles of the Labor Charter, were received by the labor leaders of Japan with high enthusiasm.

Early in the summer of 1919, the forerunners of the labor-union movement in Japan, such as Suzuki, the President of Yu-ai Kai, began to look forward to the sending of their representatives to the conference, in view of the provisions of article 389 of the Peace Treaty—which requires each government, in selecting the non-government delegates, to consult organizations which are " most representative of employers or work people." The government of Japan, on the other hand, having paid little attention to the organiza-

[1] See the translation of the entire article, *Prov. Rec.*, p. 426; see also *The Labor Movement in Japan* by S. Katayama.

tion of labor, and having consequently settled upon no definite policy heretofore as to its treatment, was the first to experience the difficulty of the situation. If the government consulted Yu-ai Kai or any other labor union (of which there were very few, the total membership of the five embryonic unions in 1919 being less than 30,000), that would be tantamount to the official recognition of labor unions. Such a course, it was feared, would not only result in the undoing of the policies of police regulation but might even fan the fire of labor and socialistic propaganda which had already been kindled.

The result of all this was seen in the elaborate "scheme of multiple election" (*Fuku-Senkio Hō*) which the government devised in order to grant voice not only to the few organized but also to the vast unorganized workers of the empire in choosing the labor representative of Japan.[1] The recourse taken to this ingenious device enabled the government, temporarily at least, to stave off the question of recognition of labor organization, because no one apparently knew whether a member or non-member of a labor union was to be elected. Finally, in September, the so-called General Conference of Labor Representatives was called in Tokio by the vice-Minister of Agriculture and Commerce. To this assembly came the delegates who were elected in all localities of the country by the aforesaid method of "multiple election," in order, as it was directed by the government, to elect the labor representative. But this assembly proved an ill-fated enterprise. From the first minute of the conference protests were raised by the union men against the alleged interference of the government in selecting the delegates. It was found that less than one-third of the delegates present were really workers themselves, and it

[1] See the report of the Committee on Credentials, clause 5, p. 5 of the *Prov. Rec.*, 7th day, Nov. 6, 1919.

was claimed that the representative of labor must be a manual worker who toils and not a non-laborer who only theorizes. Sharp questions were raised as to whether or not labor organizations were recognized. On the first day of the conference, Suzuki left the assembly in protest and he was followed by several others. The discussion lasted three days and finally Uhei Masumoto, the chief engineer as well as the director of a Japanese ship-building company, was chosen. That such a choice was not altogether fortunate is clear from the following description:[1]

This remarkable transformation of a man—from a high priest of capital to a champion of labor—created a sensation throughout the land. Some thought it to be a national scandal. A savage storm of protests accompanied Mr. Masumoto's nomination, and grew in force and fury after his acceptance of the post. Indignation meetings were held in cities and towns. There were street demonstrations and parades. On the day of Mr. Masumoto's departure a long procession of workers, clad in mourning, marched to the Yokohama wharf, waving funeral banners and chanting a dirge. Our delegate was obliged to board his ship secretly by a rope-ladder at a safe and respectful distance from the shore, *etc.*

Beyond doubt there is a bit of hyperbole in this description but it was a fact that Japan at this time was a "seething mass of unrest." The papers such as *Tokio Asahi*, *Jiji* and *Nichi-Nichi*, and the columns of current periodicals of the time were monopolized by reports or comments on the incidents of the election and sending of the labor delegate to the Washington conference. The amount of publicity given to the conference was thus unparalleled.

The seriousness with which the Japanese government regarded this conference was further attested by the extra-

[1] See "Mr. Masumoto, Japan's Labor Delegate" in *The Japan Review*, Dec., 1919, p. 43.

ordinarily large delegation which it sent. On their arrival at Seattle, they were met by the "Japanese Special" which had been despatched thither to transport these fifty-odd delegates, advisors, secretaries, interpreters and other official and unofficial force of attachés,[1] across the continent to the capital, calculated to arrive at Washington on the very day and hour of the opening of the conference. But uncertainty as to the position of the representative of Japanese labor still confronted the delegation.

The delegation, on their arrival at the Capital, were informed that protest had been raised by Mr. Gompers about the qualification of the labor representative from Japan. Thus they were greeted with the omen of battling difficulties which were to involve them till the last day of the conference.

The protest had originally been raised by Bunji Suzuki, the President of Yu-ai Kai and others who sent their letter of complaint to Samuel Gompers, and the latter submitted the communication to the conference. The matter was referred to the Committee on Credentials, and subsequently the committee, after examining the case upon the basis of the explanation given by the government delegates, reported back to the conference on November 6, that "no action should be taken on the protest in respect of the Japanese delegation."[2] However the matter was not allowed to rest. Corneille Mertens of Belgium presented a resolution in which "the workers' delegations to the International Conference at Washingotn noted the *absence* of the official workers' delegate for Japan." and this was adopted.[3] Nor

[1] A group of more than 20 men, representing the silk and other financial interests of Japan, accompanied the delegation all the way to Washington. Beside them, there were again more than 20 Japanese newspaper men assembled in Washington.

[2] See *Prov. Rec.*, p. 84.

[3] *Ibid.*, p. 79.

was the committee's report unanimous in recognizing the qualification of this delegate. Jean Oudegeest had it recorded in the report as a member of the committee, that "in future the labor delegate should be chosen in agreement with trades unions of Japan."

Suzuki's protest had its effect. The labor-union movement in Japan has gained here a foundation-stone for its future structure.[1]

4. *The Committee on Special Countries; the convention applying to Japan*

It was obvious without going into minute study of the industrial, climatic, social and other conditions of each country, that a number of countries had to be granted special consideration by the conference. Henceforth a commission originally designated as the "Committee on Tropical Countries" was appointed by the governing body with the unanimous consent of the conference,[2] to consider the matter. That the need of such an action by the conference had been contemplated is clear by referring to the provisions of the Peace Treaty. Under the "General Principles" of the Labor charter (art. 427, paragraph 2), the treaty states in explicit terms that the signatories to the covenant "recognize that differences of climate, habits and customs, of economic opportunity and industrial tradition, make strict uniformity in the conditions of labor difficult of immediate attainment." Hence the task of the committee was to carry into effect this principle of "recognition of differences." Elsewhere in the treaty, it is specifically provided that:

[1] Since then a bill to legalize and to subject trade unions to governmental control with sundry statutory restrictions has been prepared by the government of Japan. The bill will be presented to the Parliament at its coming session.

[2] See *Prov. Rec.*, p. 111.

in framing any recommendation or draft convention, the conference shall have due regard to those countries in which climatic conditions, the imperfect development of industrial organization, or other special circumstances make the industrial conditions substantially different and shall suggest the modifications, if any, which it considers may be required to meet the case of such countries.[1]

Membership on the committee was on the basis of granting full representation to the countries principally concerned and of adding three government, three employers' and three workers' delegates from non-tropical countries. The committee was constituted as follows: China 1 (g.); India 3 (g., e. and w.) Japan 3 (g., e. and w.); Siam 1 (g.); South Africa 3 (g., e. and w.); tropical America 3 (g., e. and w.), together with the following delegates from other countries: Mr. Barnes, Baron Mayor des Planches, Dr. Sulzer, Mr. Marjoribanks, Mr. Guerin, Mr. Zagleniczny, Mr. Oudegeest, Mr. Baldesi and Mr. Stuart-Bunning. Certain of these members sent their substitutes to the meetings, but in view of the importance of the decisions of the committee, Japan took this committee most seriously and Dr. Oka, the government delegate, and Sanji Muto, the employers' delegate, came in person, while the workers' delegate was represented by a substitute, a graduate of the Imperial University of Japan. India and South Africa were no less concerned about the committee's deliberations. All their delegates were present at all sessions.

Early during the conference strong objection was expressed among the Japanese labor delegates to being included among the "undeveloped," "backward" countries. Here the national or racial pride was alloyed with the economic interest of the laboring class. To keep Japan from inclusion among the special countries meant winning the

[1] Article 405, clause 3, of the Peace Treaty.

struggle for shorter working hours. If the labor delegate succeed in preventing Japan from being treated as a "special country" by this committee, that would virtually mean the eight-hour day for the workers in Japan, on the one hand, and, on the other, the retention of the claim, which Japan must assert, that Japan *is not* inferior industrially to other powers any more than in the spheres of political, military or educational achievements.

On account of the designation "Committee on Tropical Countries," the Japanese labor delegate insisted that "Japan is not a tropical country, but is similar to Italy, Spain and the United States." [1] Quoting from Huntington's *Civilization and Climate,* he maintained that "Japan lies in a zone favorable to her industrial activities, not unlike North America and Europe"; hence it was ridiculous to include Japan in this group of special countries. The labor element of the delegation designated this committee as "Eta-mura," or the Outcast-community, "Eta" being the most detested and despised social outcasts in Japan and their name the synonym for an object of scandal.

However, at the first meeting of the Committee, it was proposed that the name of the Committee should be altered and that it should thenceforth be called the "Committee on Special Countries." Without objection, the proposal, apparently innocent, was adopted; the result was that Japan, a non-tropical country, had as much right as a tropical country to remain in the group, as long as she claimed that special conditions existed in Japan.

The Committee held 14 sessions altogether, and each session was a scene of acrimonious debate.[2] In spite of

[1] See The Minority Report presented by Shichiro Muto, substitute for the labor delegate from Japan, *Prov. Rec.*, p. 325.

[2] The best reference for this committee's proceedings is the *Report* by Prof. H. W. Hetherington, Secretary of the Committee on Special Countries.

the admirable efforts of the chairman, George N. Barnes, the Committee failed to arrive at complete unanimity. The claim of the Japanese labor delegate that Japan should *not be* treated as a special country came as the minority report to the plenary session of the conference. The wholehearted support of the European labor delegates was enlisted in favor of the minority report and they demonstrated their solidarity when the conference took up the majority and minority reports for deliberation on November 27.[1] The united attack on Japan by all the leading European labor delegates and their protest against granting her specially longer hours than other industrial nations, lasted for nearly four hours while the government delegates rebutted at length.[2] The situation was finally relieved by the strong and appealing speech made by the reporter, George N. Barnes, who eloquently demonstrated the injustice of forcing the eight-hour day upon Japanese Industry. The situation was tense and dramatic; finally the majority report was adopted by the close vote of 45 to 43.

The majority report of the committee, which was adopted, recommended that Japan be granted a "delay" of five years for applying the provisions of the main convention. In the meantime the following modifications were adopted: Coal mining and work in the quarries must be immediately brought under the main convention, but for the silk industry a 60-hour week is allowed, while all other industries "might be operated on a basis of a 9½-hour daily maximum or a 57-hour week." It is further provided that a factory, to be brought within the scope of the Factory Law, should be one employing 10 persons or more instead of 15 as hitherto provided. The 48-hour week must

[1] See *Prov. Rec.*, pp. 423-432, 19th day, Nov. 27, 1919.

[2] See the drastic motion presented by Jouhaux, Oudegeest and Mertens, *Prov. Rec.*, p. 468, 20th day, Nov. 28, 1919.

also apply to children under 15 years of age. Furthermore a weekly rest period of 24 consecutive hours must be universally provided; and overtime must be arranged for in conformity to the provisions of the main convention.[1]

5. *India's case; convention applying to India*

It can be summarily stated that the greatest difficulty which is encountered by conferences of this description does not, as may be commonly expected, come from countries which are totally undeveloped. On the contrary, inasmuch as the endeavor of a conference is to set up a standard applicable to as many of the countries participating in the standardization as is practicable, on the democratic basis of equality, either the totally undeveloped or the extremely advanced are excluded from consideration as a whole and the difficulty is experienced in adjusting the claims of the countries where industry is only partially developed or where the development is in a transition stage from unorganized family industry to the modern factory system. The lack of experience in labor legislation, the insecure and inadequate equipment for the administration of protective laws, the absence of organization of labor and capital with power to prosecute efficiently agreements as to standards of hours, wages and conditions of work; these are the common features found in the countries in the Orient, in the tropics and in places where the factory system of production is not widely developed. India is no exception from this general rule.[2]

[1] See article 9, a-h of the Draft Convention on the Hours of Work.

[2] See the *Foundation of the Indian Economics* by R. Mukerjee. The author of this voluminous work denies that India is industrially undeveloped. Instead, he sets forth a claim that India has developed her industry along the lines peculiar to herself which are normal and unlike the materialistic development of the west.

Due to the absence of organized labor, the delegate sent to the conference as representative of labor in India was such practically only in name and therefore was without the authority, or the authoritative background, which other labor delegates possessed with the backing of the organized millions of workers in their respective countries. This was an obvious handicap on the part of the Indian labor delegate although his zeal and sincere efforts to promote the best interests of his fellow toilers at home were admirably demonstrated on various occasions. Statements made by W. V. Joshi, the representative of Indian labor at the meetings of the Committee on Special Countries were challenged and contradicted by both the employers' and government delegates who asserted that the vast majority of workers in India would not accept Mr. Joshi's statements. In such cases, Mr. Joshi would simply state that in his "opinion," the workers in India would want shorter hours, better wages and such conditions of work as he proposed.

In considering the case of India as a "special country" to which modifications of the main convention should apply, the committee had the advantage of access to a good deal of information regarding industrial conditions, officially supplied by the Indian government.[1] In addition the government, employers' and workers' delegates supplied abundance of information, pertinent to the question of hours of work, but even all this information could not be considered complete or even adequate to permit of a final decision as to what should be done to India. The immense size of the country and the wide differences in the conditions obtaining in the various provinces made it difficult

[1] This information is found in *Report iv*, appendix A, pp. 27-33, of the Organizing Committee to the International Labor Conference. Published September, 1919, Govt. Ptg. Office, Washington, D. C.

to generalize the situation or to apply any uniform standard. The outstanding feature was not so much the absence of industries, as the limited number of industries sufficiently organized to justify limitations of any kind. Thus, to use the expression of the Committee's report, "in India conditions do not approximate to anything which is known in the western world." [1]

Nevertheless, generally speaking, it is safe to assume that the total number of workers employed in industry in India, including factories, mines, railways, *etc.*, is relatively small,[2] the predominant occupation being agriculture, which is carried on usually on a small scale. So far as the figures available show, there were in 1915 only 1,135,147 persons employed in industry, including both the public and private establishments coming under the operation of the Factory Act of 1911. When we consider that the total population of India is safely above 300,000,000, this small number is insignificant. Of this number, 99,291 were employed in 171 establishments under either the government or other public bodies, while 1,035,856 were employed in private companies or by individuals. According to the Memorandum presented by M. R. Murray, the employers' delegate from India, the latest available figures showed that during 1918, the average number of workers employed in and about the mines regulated by the Indian Mines Act was 237,738. He claimed that "the total number of workers in organized industry and mines together would therefore amount to only 0.4% of the people of India."

[1] See column 2, pp. 323, of the *Provisional Record*, 16th day, Nov. 24, 1919.

[2] The best authority on this subject is the *Report of the Director of Statistics*, the last copy of which is dated "Calcutta, March 14, 1918." This is the only publication which attempts to give figures regarding the number of workers employed in industrial undertakings. The figures are for 1915 only and cover only the factories coming under the Indian Factory Act of 1911. Mines are excluded.

Considering now the "industrial" undertakings: in 1915 there were 279 cotton spinning and weaving mills employing 274,467 workers and 73 jute mills with 251,173 workers. As for the remaining 3701 establishments with a total of 609,507 workers, the average per establishment would amount to only 164 employees. It should be noted in this connection that these figures include cotton ginning and jute pressing, both of which are seasonal occupations employing as many as 154,668 persons during the harvesting of the cotton and jute crops. Leaving aside for a while the cotton and jute industries, there are only 454,839 workers engaged in railways, engineering workshops, iron and brass foundries, rice mills, printing presses, arsenals, dockyards, sugar and tobacco factories and other works of various descriptions.

In 1917, this being the most recent date for which the information is available,[1] there were 1,076,201 persons employed in factories in the twelve provinces of India coming under the operation of the Indian Factory Act.[2] Of these workers 907,103 or 84% were males and 169,098 or only 16% were females. 857,221 were men and 158,644 were women, making altogether 1,015,865 or over 94% adults while 60,336 or barely 6% were children under the age of 14 years.

Under such circumstances, even if other considerations were temporarily suspended, it would seem that the rigid application of the 8-hour day to India should not be considered a pressing issue. A brief examination of the legis-

[1] Here the statement and figures are based on the Memorandum submitted by A. R. Murray, Indian Employers' Delegate, p. 2. For complete information, see *Annual Report of the Director of Statistics*, Calcutta, 1917.

[2] The present Indian Factory Act applies to establishments employing 50 or more persons. It may be extended to those where 20 persons are employed if they are found to be abusive to the workers.

lative experience of India on the question of working hours and labor protection in general, reveals further the difficulty which India would encounter if rigid restrictions were imposed.[1] The first Indian Factory Act passed in 1881 did not attempt to regulate the working hours of adults but merely limited the hours of work of children and provided for the safety of workers and the inspection of work places. Ten years later (1891) another Act was passed, limiting the working day of women to 11 hours and providing a compulsory mid-day rest period and a weekly rest day. A Factory Commission, appointed in 1890, reported that the restriction on the hours of work made no improvement because "the workers themselves did not desire any change as factories worked during daylight only, the average working day being twelve hours."

The situation underwent a rapid change as electricity was introduced but the Factory Commission of 1908 was "opposed strongly to any direct limitation of working hours on the ground that the growth of industrial enterprise would be seriously hampered." The commission then advocated only the restriction of the working hours of women and children. However, the government of India went further than the recommendations of this commission and decided to limit the working hours of adult male workers in textile industries. The present Factory law has been in force since its inactment in 1911. It regulates the industries (except mines, electrical generating stations and tea, coffee and indigo plantations) in which power is used and 50 or more persons are employed. The maximum working day prescribed by the present Act is 12 hours for men in textile factories, 11 hours for women, 6 hours for children under 14 years of age in textile industry and 7 hours for children

[1] See *Memorandum* submitted to the Committee on Special Countries by L. J. Kershaw, the government delegate for India, Nov. 13, 1919.

under 14 in other industries. A compulsory rest period of an hour after 6 hours work is provided; work on Sunday is prohibited; also the employment of women and children between 7:00 p. m. and 5:30 a. m. is prohibited. Except upon approval by the government as to the shift system in force, no textile factory may be run for more than 12 hours.

These are merely legal provisions. The actual working day varies considerably. In jute mills of Bengal, employing a quarter of a million workers, more than 60% of the operatives work from 8 to 9½ hours; the weavers work 11½ hours. In upper India the cotton mills now work 11 hours, and other textile mills between 9½ and 10½ hours depending upon the season.

Aside from the consideration of working hours based on statistical figures, it must be remembered, as the Indian government delegate said.[1] that "climatic conditions are the decisive factor in determining the hour-limit and in India the ordinary operative owing to this cause is incapable of intensive or continuous work; his natural tendency at present being to spread his work over a long period, finishing his task in the most leisurely manner." "This" he says further, "is the chief characteristic of Indian labor and the most striking feature of the factory system is the amount of absence from work which is permitted to take place during the working hours. In some cases regular reliefs are arranged; in others under a ticket system provision is made for the continuous absence of a certain percentage of the workers; while in other cases, notably in the Bombay mills, the hands come and go as they please." Due to such circumstances it is claimed that "in a textile factory for instance the complements of workers must be always from 10 to 15% more than the number of hands required to man the machinery at any one time."

[1] *Ibid.*, p. 2, clause 4.

The situation just described helps to explain the divergence of claims presented by the delegates representing the opposing interests of the employers and workers as well as the amazing conservatism of the government.

The government delegate from India admitted that "12 hours is excessive" and declared that his government having adopted a "progressive policy" recently as the result of the findings of the commission of 1918, was "prepared to consent to the principle of a 60 hour week." However, he could not accept the definition of "industrial undertakings" suggested by the Organizing Committee.[1] He must enlarge the exception clause or else the overtime arrangement must be modified. He stated that the government of India was considering the obtaining of fuller statistical information in 1921. In the meantime, he was reluctant even to accept the suggestion of the 60-hour week. He would not commit himself to anything which might bind the government until the government found out what could be done.

The view of the employers' delegate was no less conservative. He said: "I feel strongly that *nothing should be done* at this conference which may have the effect of binding India to any particular course of action until such time as the enquiries now on foot have been completed." [2] After citing most minutely the present conditions of labor and the possible consequences of unemployment and other disasters in the event of any action forced upon India, the employers' delegate strongly opposed any attempt to bind India in the form of convention or treaty. In conclusion he said:

[1] *Ibid.*, clauses 5-6, p. 3.

[2] *Memorandum* submitted by A. R. Murray to the Committee on Special Countries, p. 5.

I take it upon myself to claim on behalf of Employers of Labor in India that the enquiries instituted by the government of India should be completed and all the facts taken into consideration before asking them to agree to any amendment of the present Factory Act. I therefore suggest that the whole matter be referred back to India, *etc.*[1]

The labor delegate's position could not well be radically progressive. In his final declaration on the hours question for India, the main part of his statement ran as follows:

My individual view is that *no harm* will be done to the industries in India even if the principle of 8 hours a day be introduced there immediately. *But I admit this view* will be supported neither by the employers, nor by the government, *nor by a large volume of public opinion in my country.* Therefore for practical considerations *I accept temporarily* the position that India should be excluded for some period from the application of the principle of 8 hours a day. . . .[2]

Taking all these complex circumstances and claims into consideration, the Committee refrained from making any radical suggestion in its report. It expressed the moderate opinion that the present conference could legislate usefully only with regard to such industries and mines as are under the operation of the present Indian Factory Act. The committee recommended that the government of India should be asked to apply the principle of 60 hours a week to the industries under the factory law. The committee recommended further that the conference lay before the Indian government an urgent request that it should consider first the lowering of the limit for underground work in mines

[1] *Ibid.*, p. 6.

[2] Statement submitted by W. V. Joshi, Representative of Indian labor, to the Committee on Special Countries, Nov. 14, 1919. Paragraph 1, see also *Prov. Rec.*, pp. 466-467.

and secondly the modification of the definition of "factory" to include workplaces employing less than the present limit.[1]

6. *The cases of China, Siam, Persia, South Africa and Tropical America*

The difficulty which was presented by the rest of the "special" countries was, so far as this conference at Washington was concerned, less in magnitude although there is a prospect that in no distant future the problem will grow in these countries to be much more formidable.

The lack of reliable information on these countries was one dominant cause for the limited amount of controversy about them, and their obviously low state of industrial development was another. Because of these two general reasons no far-reaching recommendations were made touching the rest of the "special" or "tropical" countries.

In the case of China, the Japanese employers' delegate stated that in certain parts of China industry was in need of legislative control. The government delegate from Japan also pointed out that China's recent industrial development called for immediate legislation and he proposed that China should be requested to adopt the same labor laws as Japan. The underlying motive for making such suggestions for China may be variously interpreted but it would be decidedly unjust to ascribe the motive entirely to economic considerations on the part of Japan growing out of a possible fear of China's competition in case Japan adopted restriction on working hours and China did not.

However, the Chinese delegate, whose progressive attitude on labor problems was undoubted, being a graduate of a celebrated American University,[2] opposed on this occasion

[1] See *Prov. Rec.*, p. 324, column 1.

[2] The Chinese delegate was Mr. Yung-Chin Yang, chancellor of the Chinese Legation at Washington, a brilliant young man and a graduate of Wisconsin University.

all suggestions of legislative restrictions for China. Even the persuasive efforts of Mr. Barnes, who suggested various broad types of labor laws along lenient and even loose lines to be applied only gradually to China, were firmly though graciously opposed. China would rather admit frankly the fact of the undeveloped status of her industries than accept the "terms" proposed by Japan, England or any other power.

The delegate of the Chinese government asked the Committee to delay framing any recommendation on the subject of China for some time. The reasons presented were that: (1) China is still very largely an undeveloped country; (2) the factory system has not grown yet to any appreciable extent there and her population is not industrialized; (3) she has had no experience with labor legislation; (4) the difficulties of administering any law at present or in the immediate future will be insurmountable because of the vast extent of the territory which is not under uniform control; (4) the Chinese government does not possess tariff autonomy, hence the difficulty of legislative control; (5) there exists a large number of foreign settlements within her territory to which the Chinese law cannot be extended, *etc.*

While recognizing these difficulties,[1] the committee in its final report to the plenary session attached "great importance to the acceptance by the Chinese government of the principle of the protection of labor by factory legislation." It suggested further, that a "beginning should be made as soon as possible in the framing and administration of such legislation" with reference to such Chinese industries as are already organized upon the modern system of production. The committee also recommended that the conference

[1] See *Prov. Rec.*, p. 324, 16th day, Nov. 24, 1919.

suggest to the Chinese government that a report be made to the next conference as to how far China is prepared to apply legislation for labor protection. For the consideration of the Chinese government the committee suggested the possibility of adopting a 10-hour day or a 60-hour week for adult workers and an 8-hour day or 48-hour week for children under 15 years of age and the system of a weekly rest day. The employment of 100 or more workers was suggested as the limit for the scope of application of labor laws. Finally the committee suggested on behalf of the Chinese government, recognizing her difficulties in connection with the existence of "extra-territoriality" in China, that the governments concerned should be asked by the conference to decree either that in their settlements or leased territories the same law should operate as in China or that the Chinese labor law should be extended to those territories.

The question of the application of the 8-hour convention to Persia and Siam was disposed of without difficulty, because it became instantly clear that in both countries, especially in Persia industry was still at a low level of development. Moreover the information obtained in regard to those countries was not felt to be sufficiently exact.[1] Therefore the committee suggested that "at the moment the convention cannot be applied to either country and that the government of these two countries should adopt the principle of labor legislation and with that in view they should collect information in the coming year and submit it to the next International Labor Conference."

The case of South Africa was still simpler and more easily disposed of because all the delegates from that country were willing to accept the main convention, at least temporarily. They felt only that in the case of a few industries, such as

[1] See *Report iv* of the Organizing Committee, Appendix B, pp. 35-37.

coal mining, sugar refining, *etc.*, in which a similar type of workers to those employed in the same industries in the East were engaged, working longer hours than usual, certain modifications might be found necessary on the maximum number of weekly hours. The views expressed by the South African delegates were agreed to by all the members of the committee and therefore no recommendation was made except the request to the government of South Africa that it " lay before the next conference a statement as to the modifications which it desires to adopt." [1]

The case of tropical America involved the difficulties naturally to be expected on account of the climatic conditions of these countries. In the sugar industry, for example, the preparation of the cane for pressing must be completed within 24 hours after it has been cut in order to arrest its deterioration. The process involves much factory and chemical handling which is mainly done by the migrant labor during the harvest season. The report of the committee simply stated that the solution of the difficulty was " entirely within the jurisdiction of the competent national authority." Hence it was unnecessary for the committee to take any action.

7. *The convention on unemployment; the " raw material " issue; the " reciprocity " question*

The second item on the agenda, viz.: " Preventing or providing against unemployment " was referred by the plenary session of the conference on November 3 to a commission of thirty members for intensive study. The conference then referred also to this commission the investigation of a subject submitted by Gino Baldesi, the Italian labor delegate, " the principle of equality of treatment on a reciprocal basis of foreign and native workers."

[1] *Ibid.*, p. 325.

The magnitude and complexity of the problem was soon realized and consequently the Commission was separated into three sub-committees. The first sub-committee, under the chairmanship of Max Lazard, the French government delegate, undertook to solve the questions relating to systematic observation and prevention of unemployment. The second sub-committee attacked the problem of the unemployed, their protection through employment agencies, and unemployment insurance. Finally the third sub-committee, under Viscount de Eza, took up the question of immigration in connection with the problem of unemployment.[1]

To these committees many proposals and counter-proposals, supported by radical and conservative views were presented. A study of them and of the manner in which they were dealt with throws a light on the psychology of the labor man which is both interesting and instructive. However space permits only a brief outline of the decisions finally reached.

The final report of the entire commission was a compilation of the decisions which were separately arrived at by the three sub-committees.[2] It consisted of six chapters, dealing with: (1) The collection and publication of information; (2) Employment; (3) Insurance against unemployment; (4) The distribution of public works; (5) Protection for unemployed foreign workers; (6) Reciprocity in treatment of foreign workers.

The report of the committee which was presented to the conference on November 22, and was subsequently adopted

[1] See *Prov. Rec.*, pp. 292-297, 15th day, Nov. 22, 1919. For a brief summary, see *The Monthly Labor Review*, Jan., 1920, pp. 12-15.

[2] Only mimeographed or typewritten records of the proceedings of these subcommittees are available. The Japanese government has prepared reports of the proceedings of all committee meetings at the conference. However, they are in Japanese only.

contained in the first place[1] a draft convention divided into three articles dealing, respectively, with statistics, employment and reciprocity in the question of insurance against unemployment. These articles provided in general that the states adhering to the convention should communicate to the International Labor Office at intervals of not more than three months all available information on unemployment and measures taken to prevent it. The various States must establish a system of free employment exchanges under the management or supervision of the Central government. Committees made up of employers and workers shall act in the capacity of advisors in the administration of these offices. These employment exchanges must furthermore be coördinated by the International Labor Office. There is also a provision in the convention that in the States ratifying it, the workers either foreign or native should receive benefits from established unemployment insurance systems upon terms agreed to by the states concerned.

Secondly[2] the report contained a draft recommendation embodying four matters, two of which dealt with the employment of workers, one with insurance against unemployment, and one with work undertaken by or on behalf of public authorities. It was recommended therein that the establishment of employment agencies charging fees should be prohibited, that the agencies of this description already in existence should operate only under licences but that the States should undertake to abolish them as soon as practicable. Further it was recommended that the recruiting of workers in one of the States in order to have them employed in another should be prohibited except upon mutual agreement by the countries concerned and after consultation

[1] See *Prov. Rec.*, p. 295, 15th day, Nov. 22, 1919.

[2] *Ibid.*

with both the employers and workers concerned in the same industries. State unemployment insurance systems were also recommended, and the coördination of public works in order "to reserve as far as practicable the work in question for periods of unemployment and for districts most affected by such unemployment."

In the third place four resolutions were addressed to the governing body of the International Labor Office. These related to the means of collecting and publishing information on unemployment, and regarding agricultural workers. In connection with agriculture it was provided that the International Labor Office should establish relationship with the International Institute of Agriculture at Rome so as to secure from the latter information on agricultural unemployment. Touching upon the question of migration and protection of foreign workers, the committee was of the opinion that due regard should be given to the sovereignty of each country and the resolution was simply for the International Commission "to report upon measures for the protection of such workers."

Finally the report of the committee contained a special convention which seemed somewhat drastic to certain of the delegates, namely the provision on "reciprocity in the treatment of foreign workers in all matters relating to the protection of labor." The convention stated that:

> . . . the States ratifying this convention or acceding to it shall reciprocally admit to the benefit of the laws and regulations having regard to labor protection, as well as the right of lawful organization, the workers belonging to one of these states and employed in another, together with their families.[1]

When the conference reached this point in the course of its deliberations, a considerable divergence of opinion among

[1] *Ibid.*, p. 296.

the delegates developed before the conference finally adopted the proposition. But the most debated issue was on the minority report on the motion offered originally by Gino Baldesi, the Italian workers' delegate, dealing with the "equitable distribution of raw materials as a means of preventing unemployment." When this matter was originally presented before the sub-committee, the proposition was rejected by the majority of the committee on the ground that it was not within its jurisdiction to discuss such economic problems which have a political character. The minority, headed by Baldesi and supported by other labor members of the committee, disagreed and maintained that it was entirely within the competence of the conference, and hence of the committee, to deal with this important cause of unemployment. It held that practical steps must be suggested by the responsible committee to deal with the problem of improving the distribution of raw materials among the several countries.

The contention of the minority on this question proceeded from the economic viewpoint of international interests and emphasized mainly phases of economics which have little regard for nationalistic sentiments. The proposition received the full support of such left-wing leaders of the conference as Jouhaux, Ilg, Oudegeest and Martens, while the employers were almost unanimous in opposing it. The contention of the latter was that the proposition was in effect an interference with property rights and that the International Labor Conference was not authorized to go so far, since its task was simply to improve labor conditions. After portraying the vast extent of unemployment existing and the havoc played by the war, the minority report says:

Should this abundant labor be forced to emigrate to those countries where the raw materials are to be found? Or would it not be more just and humane to make said raw materials available in those countries where labor abounds? If it is true that men should be afforded the opportunity to avoid the sorrows of exile from their native countries and that they are better and more valuable citizens the more they are attached to the land of their birth where they have grown from childhood, then the answer cannot be doubtful.[1]

In answer to the objection that the countries which are abundantly supplied with natural resources would resent such a suggestion, which amounts to interference with their freedom and right of disposing of their own possessions, the labor delegates contended that:

labor also may be considered as doubly entitled to respect as being doubly the property first of the worker himself and secondly of the country to which he belongs. Yet this has not prevented the countries here represented from desiring to see some international regulation of the conditions of human labor without feeling that in so doing they are in any sense humiliated, or that their rights are thereby infringed upon. . . .

The practical proposal of the workers' delegates for immediate action on this important question was embodied in the motion of Gino Baldesi, which was as follows:

Considering that the question of unemployment is closely related to that of the distribution of raw materials and the means of maritime transport and freight rates,—considering further that the question can only be effectively dealt with by the Council of the League of Nations, it is recommended that the council should undertake to examine and solve the problem.

Counter to this motion was another, presented by the French and Swiss employers' delegates, to the effect that the whole matter should be tabled and referred to the govern-

[1] *Ibid.*, p. 296, column 2.

ing body because of the complexity of the problem. Both this and the Baldesi motion suffered defeat.[1]

An important amendment to the draft which was finally adopted by the conference related to the membership on the international commission designed to study the regulation and protection of immigrant workers. This limited the European States to one-half of the total membership. Later in this chapter we shall deal further with the issue of the European *v.* the non-European states.

8. *Employment of women*

In considering the third item on the agenda, namely the question of the employment of women, the spirit of the labor section of the peace treaty (See articles 389, 427,-ninth principle, *etc.*) was fully recognized. The committee charged with the intensive study of this question consisted largely of women advisors, participating in the discussion either in full capacity as members of the committee or as substitutes to the delegates properly designated as members. Prominent among these women were Miss Constance Smith of Great Britain who acted as the chairman, Madame Majerova of Czecho-Slovakia, Madame Letellier and Mlle. Bonvier of France, Madame Casartelli of Italy, and Madame Tanaka of Japan.[2]

The final report of the committee was made on November 18, by Miss Constance Smith who appeared before the plenary session to make the only report presented by a woman.[3] In view of the limited time at the disposal of the

[1] See in this connection, the memorandum presented by Baron Mayor des Planches, *Prov. Rec.*, p. 467, 20th day, Nov. 28, 1919. Also draft convention proposed by Argentine, on unemployment, pp. 225-226, 13th day, Nov. 19, 1919.

[2] See for the full list of members on the committee, *Prov. Rec.*, p. 172, 11th day, Nov. 14, 1919.

[3] See *Prov. Rec.*, pp. 204-205.

committee, they took precautions to avoid proposals likely to involve prolonged discussions. The recommendations of the committee were "confined to a few points arising out of the accepted principle embodied in the convention of Berne." The committee was unanimous in accepting the principle enunciated in the Berne convention, that women in industry shall not be employed during the night. But it was considered advisable to make certain revisions "in order to make it an efficient international instrument at the present time."

The reason for calling a revision is obvious. Thirteen years had elapsed since the signing of the Berne convention and during that whole period the industrial growth of the different countries had been remarkable. Moreover the war brought about tremendous changes in the legal and economic status of the workers, especially that of women, so that it would be no exaggeration to state that the provisions of the Berne convention were already becoming out of date. Nevertheless the committee recognized that it would be futile to try to effect a modification of the convention which is in force. Accordingly the main provisions of the existing conventon were left untouched, and the committee recommended instead a "new convention concerning the night work of women to be put forth by the conference, to supersede the Berne convention of 1906." But this was of course a question of form. The task of the committee, as a matter of fact, consisted in the extension of the provisions of the Berne convention.

The old convention limited its application to undertakings employing more than 10 men or women. Thirteen years of experience through the great war and the phenomenal changes in industrial conditions made it apparent that such a broad limitation as the convention of 1906 provided was inadequate at present to safeguard the women workers. Therefore it was proposed that the limitation relative to the number of employed persons should be removed. Only the clause stating that the convention should not apply to " undertakings in which only the members of the family are employed " was retained.

In view of the necessity that the present convention should apply at least as extensively as the other conventions, the committee suggested a restatement of the definition of " industrial undertakings " so as to include all undertakings that are within the sphere of application of other conventions. This necessitated the insertion of substitute clauses in the original draft. Thus the convention would now apply to: [1]

(a) Mines and quarries and extractive industries of every kind.

(b) Industries in which articles are manufactured, altered, repaired, ornamented, finished, or adapted for sale, or broken up or demolished, or materials are transformed (including the generation, transformation, and transmission of motive power, electric, hydraulic, *etc.*, shipbuilding, laundry work).

(c) Construction, reconstruction, repair, maintenance, alteration or demolition, of any building, railway, tramway, harbor, dock, pier, canal, inland navigation, road, tunnel, bridge, viaduct, sewer, drain, well, telegraphic, telephonic installation, electrical undertaking, gas work, water work, or other work or construction and the preparation for and laying the foundation of any such work or building.

The laws of each individual country shall define the line of division which separates industry from agriculture and commerce.

There was considerable discussion on the question of what hours shall constitute the " night." The Berne con-

[1] Article I, a-c of the Draft Convention concerning employment of women during the night.

vention of 1906 prescribed that it should consist of 11 consecutive hours, comprising in it the hours between 10 p. m. and 5 a. m. Touching this there was difference of opinion in the committee, as the Italian delegate Mrs. Laura Cabrini insisted that there should be an uninterrupted night rest of 8 hours. This provision, as she pointed out, would allow the convenience of two 8-hour shifts during the remaining 16 hours. This proposition did not receive acceptance in the committee, but she submitted it as a minority report to the conference.[1]

Another dissenting opinion was expressed by the French employers' delegate who argued from the point of view of a factory manager that it was necessary to extend the period of daytime employment to last from 4 a. m. to 10 p. m., "if industry is to run without serious interruption." In consequence a motion to that effect was submitted providing in addition that the work of each shift be broken by one hour of rest. However, neither this nor the proposition of the Italian delegate was accepted and the majority report was adopted.

The convention as embodied in the majority report provides that the term " night " signifies " a period of at least eleven consecutive hours, including the interval between ten o'clock in the evening and five o'clock in the morning." In order to meet the difficulty of the countries where no government regulation has ever restricted the night work of women, the convention specifies that in such countries the term night " may provisionally, and for a maximum period of three years, be construed to signify a period of only ten hours, including the interval between ten o'clock p. m. and five o'clock a. m."[2] The benefit of this

[1] See *Prov. Rec.*, p. 227, 13th day, Nov. 29, 1919.

[2] Article 2 of the Draft Convention concerning employment of women during the night.

provision will be appreciably felt by countries like Japan where the attempt to regulate women's night work has not yet succeeded, due to industrial conditions which cannot be altered without due allowance of time for preparation. For the benefit of India and Siam it is specifically provided that the present convention "may be suspended by the government in respect to any industrial undertaking except factories as defined by the national law." [1] General exceptions to the provisions of the convention, applicable to the case of *force majeure,* seasonal industries, *etc.,* are provided in exactly the same manner as in all the other conventions adopted at this conference.

With regard to maternity protection, the conference adopted probably the most far-reaching convention. It defines, for the purpose of the present convention, the term "woman" to signify "any female person, irrespective of age or nationality, whether married or unmarried," and the term "child" signifies "any child legitimate or illegitimate." [2] The important parts of this convention are found in articles 3 and 4. Therein it is provided that a woman wage-earner, no matter whether she be engaged in an industrial or commercial establishment, should not be employed during the six weeks immediately following confinement.[3] She also has the right to leave her work six weeks before confinement, upon submitting a doctor's certificate.[4] Furthermore in case of a mistake in estimating the probable time of confinement, the convention provides that the allowance of maternity benefits should not be denied. The benefit must be paid to her in any case by the State or

[1] *Ibid.,* article 5.

[2] Article 2 of the "Draft Convention concerning the employment of women before and after childbirth."

[3] *Ibid.,* article 3 (a).

[4] *Ibid.,* article 3 (b).

by means of a system of insurance, and this maternity benefit "must be sufficient for the full and healthy maintenance of the mother and child." The woman is entitled also to free attendance by a doctor or certified midwife. The exact amount of money benefit is left for the "competent authority" in each country to determine. For the purpose of nursing, half an hour twice a day during the working hours, must be granted to women with babies.

The conference found itself in difficulty over the question whether or not commercial undertakings should be included; Leon Jouhaux asserted that two-thirds of women wage-earners are engaged in commercial and not industrial establishments, and it would therefore be ridiculous not to include commercial undertakings within the scope of the convention if the purpose of the convention is to protect wage-earning women. The force of this argument was convincing although in view of the difficulty of enforcement the government delegates invariably showed reluctance to commit themselves to such a sweeping convention. It should be noted that this was the only convention where "commercial undertakings" were brought in. The rest of the convention adopted at the Washington Conference applied exclusively to industry. This was, therefore, highly progressive legislation.

9. *Employment of children*

The fourth item on the agenda, *viz.*, the employment of children, was referred to a committee of twenty-one members, which labored on the questions of minimum age of admission and children's night work.[1] The final report of the committee to the plenary session was made by Sir Malcolm Delevigne, chairman of the committee, who presented to the conference a draft convention attached to the report.[2]

[1] See *Prov. Rec.*, p. 172, 11th day, Nov. 14, 1919.

[2] *Ibid.*, pp. 187-188, 12th day, Nov. 17, 1919.

The substance of the convention proposed by the Committee was identical with the draft prepared by the Organizing Committee except for slight modifications. The committee, according to the report, was " unanimous " in accepting the age of 14 as the minimum age of admission of children into industrial work.[1]

In preparing the draft the committee had in view the object of making the convention " an advance over existing conditions within practical limits." There were proposals at the committee meetings to raise the age limit to 15, and 16; also there were those who advocated the extension of the scope of the convention to agriculture and commerce, but the majority of the committee prevailed over the undue idealism of the minority. Consequently the matter of extension of the application was simply set forth in the report as a recommendation that " the conference should pronounce in favor of the limitation of the age of admission to agricultural, commercial, and other occupations. . . ."

Differences arose in the committee with regard to the date of enforcement of the convention. The Belgian and Spanish employers and the Italian government delegates contended that there should be a longer period of preparation allowed. In Italy, Greece and elsewhere the age of completion of the elementary education is lower than 14, and it was urged that January 1, 1922, which the convention set as the date for the convention to go into effect, would hardly allow sufficient time to rearrange the educational system. It was pointed out by the workers' delegates that the treaty allows 12 months within which each government should present the draft convention to the legislature of the nation and therefore the provisions should be brought into practice by January 1, 1921. On this basis they contended

[1] See Article 2 of the " Draft Convention fixing the minimum age for admission of children to industrial employment."

that the date of enforcement should be fixed at January 1, 1921.[1]

This matter was disposed of by a vote of 10 to 5. The real difficulty was in establishing the minimum age for the Oriental countries. A sub-committee was formed to study the situation more intensively and as the result the following modifications were made:

In the case of Japan it was agreed that the minimum age should be 14 but children above 12 could be admitted into industrial work if they have completed their elementary education.[2] As for India and other countries the committee did not submit any recommendation, but the conference inserted in the convention[3] that children under 12 years of age should not be employed in India in manufactories working with power and employing more than ten persons, nor in mines, quarries and certain other industries. The adoption of such an amendment on behalf of the Indian workers was the result largely of the convincing manner in which Miss Margaret Bonfield of Great Britain put the proposition. It was opposed vigorously by Chatterjee, the government delegate from India; but Joshi the workers' delegate gave his support to the amendment.

The matter of prohibition of night work of young persons received also full consideration by the same committee and report on this subject was made to the plenary session of the conference on November 24.[4]

The basis upon which this committee worked was the Berne convention of 1913, which had not been formally ratified on account of the war. Beside this the committee had before it the draft convention prepared by the Organizing

[1] *Ibid.*, article 11.

[2] *Ibid.*, article 5.

[3] *Ibid.*, article 6.

[4] *Prov. Rec.*, pp. 326-328, Nov. 24, 1919.

Committee.[1] The age at which a young person may be allowed to work during the night, the Berne convention of 1913 had fixed at 16 years. But the draft of the Organizing Committee raised it to 18 and the present committee adopted the latter, i. e. 18, in preference to the former.

According to the convention finally adopted the period of night rest is defined as comprising 11 consecutive hours, including the period between 10 p. m. and 5 a. m.[2] The universal age-limit of 18 may be lowered to 16 in the industries which require a continuous prosecution of work, day and night, to avoid waste of fuel or rapid deterioration of material. This exception extends to manufacture of iron and steel, glass-works, manufacture of paper, raw sugar, gold mining, *etc.* The prohibition of night work for young persons over 16 years of age may be suspended if the public interest so requires, or in case an emergency arises which the employer could not control or foresee, and which is not of a periodic character. An interesting exception, provided for in the convention, is that in bakeries where night work is prohibited, the hours 9 p. m. to 4 a. m., instead of 10 p. m. to 5 a. m., may be substituted as the period of night rest.

However, still more interesting than this was the ground upon which Japan demanded, and succeeded in obtaining, exemption from the main convention. According to the testimony of Dr. A. Kose, the medical advisor to the Japanese delegation, " it has been demonstrated that the Japanese are, generally speaking, a race tending to premature development." As " the reason for fixing the age limit of the minors at 16 years and under," the government dele-

[1] See *Report iii* of the Organizing Committee, pp. 53-55.

[2] Article 3 of the Draft Convention concerning the night work of young persons employed in industry.

gate from Japan submitted a statement which reads in part as follows:[1]

The period of pubertic development of a male Japanese, according to medical authorities, starts at the age of 12 years and lasts until the age of 16, whereas in the case of a female Japanese the period is from 11 years to 15 years of age.[2] Hence it is undoubtedly a safe policy to have 16 years of age as the age-limit for legal protection. The object of protection of the workers during the period of their physical growth and important pubertic development will be sufficiently realized by this provision.

A similar reason was presented as the ground for excluding the female workers above 16 years of age from the "class of minors under legal protection" in Japan. It was pointed out also[3] that the exclusion of the female worker above 16 years of age from this convention would not necessarily place her in a helpless position because the Japanese law prohibits the employment of women in dangerous or unhealthy processes.

Upon this ground the conference decided to adopt a convention finally in favor of Japan, granting 15 years of age for the first three years after the main convention becomes operative, and after that time 16 years of age to be substituted for the 18 years provided in the convention.[4]

[1] See "The Statement by the Japanese government delegation regarding the modification of the draft convention on the hours of work" submitted to the Committee on Special Countries, Nov. 17, 1919, p. 7.

[2] "This makes the physiological growth of a Japanese, either male or female, two years earlier than that of a European. The period of pubertic development of a European is generally from 14 to 18 years of age."—Dr. A. Kose.

[3] The Statement by the Japanese Gov. Del., *loc. cit.*, p. 8.

[4] Article 5 of the "Draft Convention concerning the night work of young persons employed in industry."

In the case of India the convention applies only to the workers engaged in establishments where the Indian Factory Law is in force, and for boys, 14 years, was substituted for 18 years.[1] The convention further extended its exceptions to the cases of seasonal work, emergencies, *etc.*, as in all other conventions. This convention goes into effect on July 1, 1922.

10. *The recommendations on "unhealthy processes;" on the use of white phosphorus*

Much to the disappointment of certain delegates with technical knowledge the important matter of "unhealthy processes" was reported on by the committee in charge in the form of mere recommendations. Moreover lead and anthrax were the only subjects upon which recommendations were made.

The recommendations regarding lead poisoning were that:

in view of the danger involved to the function of maternity and to the physical development of children, women and young persons under the age of 18 years be excluded from employment in the following processes:

(a) In furnace work in the reduction of zinc or lead ores.

(b) In the manipulation, treatment or reduction of ashes containing lead and in the desilvering of lead.

(c) In melting lead or old zinc on a large scale.

(d) In the manufacture of solder or alloys containing more than 10% of lead.

(e) In the manufacture of litharge, massicot, red lead, white lead, orange lead, or sulphate, chromate or silicate (frit) of lead.

(f) In mixing and pasting, in the manufacture or repair of electric accumulators.

[1] *Ibid.*, article 6.

(g) In the cleansing of work rooms where the above processes are carried on.

Anticipating cases in which it might be necessary to modify these restrictive measures, the following conditions were recommended as essential before the employment of women and young people should be permitted:

(a) Locally applied exhaust ventilation so as to remove dust and fumes at the point of origin.

(b) Cleanliness of tools and work rooms.

(c) Notification to Government authorities of all cases of lead poisoning and compensation therefor.

(d) Periodic medical examination of the persons employed in such processes.

(e) Provision of sufficient and suitable cloak room, washing and mess room accommodation, and of special protective clothing.

(f) Prohibition of bringing food or drink into workrooms.

It was further recommended that in industries where soluble lead compounds could be replaced, by non-toxic substances, the use of soluble lead compounds should be strictly regulated. For the purpose of this recommendation, a lead compound is considered as soluble if more than five *per cent* of its weight is soluble in a quarter of one *per cent* solution of hydrochloric acid.

The recommendation concerning the prevention of anthrax, as adopted by the conference, was simple both in form and substance. It was:

the General Conference recommends to the members of the International Labor Organization that arrangements should be made for the disinfection of wool infected with anthrax spores, either in the countries exporting such wool or, if it is not practicable, at the port of entry in the country importing such wool.

There was another recommendation adopted by the conference, for the establishment of an efficient factory inspection service in each country, where it does not already exist, and also for the creation in each country of a government service whose duty it should be to safeguard the health of workers and to keep in touch with the International Labor Office.

Finally on the application of the Berne convention prohibiting the use of white phosphorus in the manufacture of matches, the conference adopted unanimously the recommendation:

that each Member of the International Labor Organization, which has not already done so, should adhere to the International Convention adopted at Berne in 1906 on the prohibition of the use of white phosphrus in the manufacture of matches.

Prior to the adoption of this recommendation, the Secretary General of the conference communicated with the government delegates of all the countries at the conference, inquiring as to their attitude on this question. Judging from the large number of favorable replies which were received by him and judging further by the unanimous adoption of this recommendation, we may rest assured that the use of white phosphorus in match-manufacture will soon become a matter unknown in the civilized world included in the League of Nations.

11. *The governing body of the International Labor Office*

In view of the large number of countries which participated in the conference with their varied economic and political interests, it was noteworthy that "politics" played so small a part in the sessions of the conference. The nearest approach to politics was perhaps on the question of membership on the governing Body of the International Labor Office. It simply happened that out of 24 members who were to constitute the Governing Body, 20 of those duly elected were from European countries and only 4 the representatives of countries outside of Europe.[1] As a result a written protest was entered by the Latin-American delegates, pointing out the apparent injustice of the choice. A careful study of the situation discloses an interesting trend of probable development in the conferences which are to follow.

In article 393 of the Peace Treaty, it is provided that of the 12 members representing the governments on the "governing body" of the international labor office, 8 shall be "nominated by the high contracting parties of chief industrial importance" and 4 by the government delegates attending the conference, who are not of the 8 countries. In accordance with this provision, at the suggestion of the committee of selection, the delegates, 36 in number, representing 29 countries which were not among the 8 nations of chief industrial importance, held meetings to select four members out of their own number to sit in the governing body. Finally the following states were selected to be represented on the governing body: Spain, Argentina, Canada, and Poland, obtaining 29, 26, 20 and 16 votes respectively, out of the possible 31 votes. Denmark and Rumania each received the next highest number of votes, which was 9, and Denmark was chosen to be the country to fill in the vacancy in the number of 12 states above mentioned in the case such vacancy should occur.

Dissatisfaction was first expressed by the delegates from India and China on the ground that the united population of these two countries was so large that they should in fairness be represented on the governing body. Later the Chin-

[1] See *Prov. Rec.*, pp. 353-354, 17th day, Nov. 25, 1919.

ese delegate declared that he would make no demand on this subject, but the Indian delegates refused to participate in the election. The claim of the Indian delegates was supported by the representatives of the Canadian, South-African, Cuban and other governments. But the above stated choice was temporarily agreed upon as the decision of the Assembly of the government Delegates and was submitted to the conference at its plenary session on November 25.

The government-members nominated to be representatives on the governing body were thus: Belgium, France, Great Britain, Italy, Japan, Germany, Switzerland, Spain, Argentina, Canada, Poland, and, pending the appointment of the United States representative, Denmark.

The employers' nominees were: Sir A. Smith, Great Britain; L. Guerin, France; Pirelli, Jr., Italy; J. Carlier. Belgium; M. Hodacz, Czecho-Slovakia and, pending the appointment of the United States employers' representative, Shindler of Switzerland. The workers' nominees were: Jouhaux, France; Oudegeest, Netherlands; Stuart-Bunning, Great Britain; Lindquist, Sweden and, pending the appointment of the United States workers' delegate, Draper of Canada. The sixth place was left for the German worker.

The choices were obviously unfair toward the countries outside of Europe. The protest of the Latin American delegates pointed out that only one (Argentina) out of 20 Latin-American republics was on this body. It was vigorously contended by them that if the composition of the governing body was "to respond sincerely to the high purposes of carrying out international aims," the conference must endeavor to make an "equitable distribution of forces within the organization." They "agreed to assert their personality before the International Labor Conference" and demanded the correction of the "injustice" of this mode of allotment, declaring their "inconformity with the distribution that has been made." [1] The Canadian delegate, Mr. Rowell, stated that caution must be taken to make this an "international" and not a "European" conference if it was to be a long enduring institution.

Here was a totally unforeseen difficulty. It forecast the friction which may arise in future conferences so long as the interests of continental Europe, or of any other geographical area seem to be guarded to the disadvantage of other regions. Furthermore this difficulty might be interpreted as indicative even of a "political" trend, running in the direction of the growing issue concerning the "rights of small nations."

Arthur Fontaine, a man of long experience in international labor affairs, explained that the present arrangement was most convenient because the governing body must meet every two months at Geneva. A delegate not belonging to a European state would find it difficult to attend the meetings. Moreover, through a system of grouping, the small countries with little or no industry might be enabled to present their case and claims through the representatives of the group.

The conference finally adopted by a vote of 44 to 39, this resolution, offered by Gemmil, employers' delegate from South Africa:

> that this conference expresses its disapproval of the composition of the governing body of the International Labor Office, inasmuch as no less than 20 out of 24 members of that body are representatives of European countries.[2]

As the provisional Director General of the International

[1] *Ibid.*

[2] See *Prov. Rec.*, p. 499, 21st day, Nov. 29, 1919.

Labor Office, Albert Thomas of France was selected by the governing body. The same body elected Arthur Fontaine chairman. The location of the office of this body was provisionally decided to be Sunderland House, Curzon St. W. London and its next meeting was arranged to be held in Paris, January 26, 1920.[1]

CONCLUSION

HAVING completed its assigned task, the conference adjourned formally on November 29, 1919. In his farewell address Secretary Wm. H. Wilson, the presiding officer said to the foreign delegates:

> . . . I am greatly impressed with the idea that you have been hewing out the blocks for the foundation of a structure to shelter the toiling masses of the future. You have worked patiently, you have brought a splendid enthusiasm, a high standard of intelligence, a thorough earnestness toward the laying of this foundation. And I am sure I express your hopes, and the hopes of the peoples of all the world, that time may develop the fact that you have built well, that you have laid the foundation for a structure that will stand down through all the ages as the protector of the toilers of the world.[2]

In contrast with what may be included in the ideal of international labor agreement, the Washington Conference was without doubt disappointing in the eyes of some radical delegates. To those extremists whose notion of international labor legislation is to set maximum standards of

[1] This meeting was held in Paris as arranged, and plans of internal organization and financial operation were made. Brief report of this meeting is found in *The New York Times*, Jan. 27 and 29, 1920. Official report is available only in typewritten form. Its second meeting is to be held in London, March 20, 1920.

[2] See *Prov. Rec.*, p. 503, 21st day.

legal protection, the conference may have seemed a failure. On the other hand, in the opinion of those men who hold it to be the function of the conference to set up immediately attainable maximums only within practicable limits, the conference was in no way a disheartening incident.[1]

Indeed the conference was a success—not because it attempted to accomplish much but because its program was modest. It is granted that the conventions and recommendations adopted there seem rather meager coupled with its high-sounding title: "the First Labor Conference under the League of Nations." Nonetheless the conference has begun the work of construction and it has unquestionably "laid the foundation for the structure." With the untold difficulties facing the conference, fatal disruption would not have been suprising. The simple fact that the conference not only reached agreement on every item of the agenda but also laid plans for its own future course of action, should be regarded as convincing proof of the practicability of the scheme. International labor legislation is no longer a mere idea; it is a reality to which man may owe his future peace, freedom and prosperity. In the solution of labor problems, which are now world-wide, international action alone is adequate to meet the difficulties which cross frontiers. The maintenance of world-peace is possible only when its economic foundations are secure; we may expect much from the conferences, where by international coöperation, mutual help is employed to allay the unrest of workers.

While few things are as hazardous as the attempt to predict the future of an institution which is just born, one

[1] See the "Opinions regarding the Conference" *Monthly Labor Review*, Jan., 1920, pp. 25-26; *New Republic*, Dec. 24, 1919, pp. 110-112; *Survey*, Nov. 15, 1919, pp. 107-108; *American Federationist*, Jan., 1920, pp. 51-56, *etc.*

thing may properly be reëmphasized in concluding this essay. The Washington conference, realizing that it was only the "beginning" of world-wide labor legislation, confined itself mainly to "laying the ground work." The real work is still ahead. The "raw material" and "reciprocity" issues were only slight indications of the storms which may assail the conference in future. The tense and serious atmosphere which was felt at all debates throughout the session, solemnly foreshadowed the development of the conference. It must be remembered that the question of collective bargaining, the obstacle upon which the first "Industrial Council" of President Wilson was seen to crumble to dust, will some time or other have to be brought up for consideration. The right of organization which is recognized in the labor charter must also be subjected to international agreement. The question of a minimum living-wage is another, and the institution of joint councils in all industries is still another. Furthermore the hours of work must be made even shorter than at present over most of the world; the minimum age of admission to work must be raised, the protection of women and children must be widened in scope and in short every effort must be made in all directions to promote the interests of society by safeguarding those who produce.[1] Thus the task for future International Labor Conferences is manifold; the work is only begun.

[1] A comprehensive list of helpful readings in this connection is: *Industrial Democracy 1848-1919—A Study Help prepared by the Library Employees Union of Greater New York, Local No. 15590, A. F. of L. Pamphlet No. 1.* See also *Democracy in Reconstruction* by Cleveland and Schafer; *Labor and Capital after the War*, by S. J. Chapman; H. Carter, *Industrial Reconstruction, etc.*

Bei Fragen zur Produktsicherheit wenden Sie sich bitte an:
If you have any questions regarding product safety,
please contact:

Walter de Gruyter GmbH
Genthiner Straße 13
10785 Berlin
productsafety@degruyterbrill.com